After graduating from high school in the late 1980s, **Peter Salten** moved from the US to Denmark for a year of study abroad. The letters he wrote to his mom while in Denmark are collected in *Adolescent Abroad*. In these open and honest letters, Peter describes his reactions to the psychological and social challenges facing a maturing adolescent, one on his own abroad, while trying to maintain a sense humor about his situation and conduct…

Marie Salten, Peter's mom, holds a graduate degree in counseling psychology. In her introduction to *Adolescent Abroad*, she describes Peter's early life, and the development of their close relationship. Marie also provides commentary for each of Peter's letters, giving factual, psychological and social context to his thoughts, feelings, experiences.

Adolescent Abroad

also from
Skaeg Books

SCHIZOPHRENIC AMERICA
by Anni Damgaard

THE POET ANDREW SKIGG
by Elbert Shamroc

SkaegBooks.com

Adolescent Abroad
Peter's Letters to Mom

Peter and Marie Salten

Skaeg Books
PHOENIX

Copyright © 2019 by Peter and Marie Salten
　All rights reserved

ISBN 978-1-945258-15-2 (hcv)
　　978-1-945258-16-9 (pbk)
　　978-1-945258-17-6 (epub)
　　978-1-945258-18-3 (azw)

Library of Congress Control Number:2019943282

Cover & Drawings © 2019 by Peter Salten
　All rights reserved

The letters in this book are memoir, based on true events. Other observers, however, may remember those events differently. All names and a few identifying details have been changed for this publication.

SkaegBooks.com

Contact: STJ@skaegbooks.com

Skaeg Books is an imprint of Skaeg Publishing LLC
Skaeg Books and the Skaeg logos are trademarks of
　Skaeg Publishing LLC

Book design by STJ – 2p

skaeg (skāg) 1. beard; 2. enjoyable, informed, cool

*Childhood memories of my mother
taught me the value of motherhood*
– Marie Salten

Contents

Introducing Peter..3
Section I. Getting Settled...11
   Letter 1 – Homesick..13
   Letter 2 – My New Pad..17
   Letter 3 – Starting School...21
   Letter 4 – A Cute Girl..29
   Letter 5 – Getting Drafted...35
   Letter 6 – New Friends..39
Section II. Choosing a Career...45
   Letter 7 – Letters from Friends....................................47
   Letter 8 – Checking-out Universities..........................55
   Postcard from Costa Brava..61
   Letter 9 – Birthday Party..65
   Letter 10 – Things Missed..69
   Letter 11 – A Sexual Encounter....................................75
   Letter 12 – Career Confusion.......................................81
   Letter 13 – Thanksgiving..87
Section III. Holiday Blues...93
   Letter 14 – The Flu..95
   Letter 15 – Nila Arrives...101
   Christmas Card...107
   Letter 16 – A Clean Shave..111
Section IV. Girls...117
   Letter 17 – Wham, Girls!...119
   Letter 18 – Grades...125
   Letter 19 – A Girlfriend...133
   Letter 20 – …A Break-up..139
   Letter 21 – Things on My Mind..................................149

Letter 22 – Winter Lingers... 155
Letter 23 – Pick-Pocket... 161
Letter 24 – Spring At Last.. 167
Section V. Winding down... 175
Letter 25 – Movies... 177
Letter 26 – Happy B.D. Mom.. 181
Letter 27 – Male Bonding... 189
Letter 28 – Senioritis, Again... 193
Letter 29 – Separation Anxiety... 199
Conclusion... 203

Adolescent Abroad

Introducing Peter

Forty-five years ago I delivered a baby in an army hospital in Texas. The nurse held the little newborn towards me so I could see that it was a boy. Then she took him away. After recovering from the shock of giving birth, I was overcome by unfamiliar feelings of responsibility and affection for my infant son. As soon as I was allowed to get out of bed, I inquired about directions to the newborn nursery. There I paced in front of a large window wondering which of the many infants belonged to me. Hospital regulations allowed mothers to have contact with their babies only during feeding times. I was restless and distressed at this involuntary separation. Finally, after eight long hours, I met Peter. We have had a deep affection for one another ever since.

When Peter and I returned to the army hospital for our first well-baby check-up, the waiting room was filled with young mothers and their infants. We waited three to four hours before we finally saw the doctor. Other mothers became restless, and some babies started to cry, but Peter and I were content. We were smiling at one another, nursing when he got hungry, just enjoying each other's company. I realized then that our relationship was special.

Peter was very active as a young child, but could be calm when appropriate. While he was still a toddler, I began attending university classes to upgrade the medical technology certification I had received in my home country, Denmark. Occasionally I brought Peter with me to class. He knew it was important to be completely quiet during lectures. He would draw with crayons while sitting on my lap, patiently waiting until the lecture ended. He never complained. In fact he seemed excited to be in a different place and experience new things.

One day when Peter was two years old, he came running to me with tears in his eyes. A splinter had worked its way under his fingernail. Calmly, I put Peter on my lap and soaked his finger in soap-water while we exchanged stories. After half and hour, I gently tweezed the splinter out. Peter watched attentively during the "operation," never crying, trusting that I was doing my very best to make his finger better.

Peter's little sister Nila arrived shortly before his third birthday. These were troubled times for Peter. When I was caring for his sister, Peter busied himself in his room. After a couple of months, I began talking to him about his little sister, and how it felt to be a big brother. Peter honestly told me that he disliked Nila. However, he said he didn't think it was right to "throw her in the garbage can." Eventually, Peter accepted his sister and their friendship grew strong. As adults, they still draw much support from each other.

Peter was seven-years-old when his father and I divorced. We were all sad, but Peter made it his responsibility to keep Nila and me smiling. He became the family entertainer, always joking and engaging us in conversation. He also became very protective of Nila and me.

Introducing Peter

During Peter's early adolescence I decided to pursue a graduate degree while continuing my work as a medical technologist. Peter took over the household chores while Nila helped with the cooking. The three of us were a close-knit team. We always talked, sharing the good things and the bad; and we learned to trust and respect one another.

Peter never got too old to kiss me hello or goodbye, even in front of his friends. There was never anything he wanted to keep secret from me. I did not completely appreciate the extent of Peter's trust in me until one day he came running to me after dinner. He had found five "would be" pubic hairs on his lower abdomen. He was so proud! I felt honored that he wanted to share this very important event with me. He was growing up, but we never grew apart.

Peter was taller and more sensitive than the majority of boys his age. Being tall somewhat compensated for his tender spirit. However, he told me that he was occasionally bullied by other boys, and he detested himself for not being tough. Throughout high school he lifted weights, and his muscular appearance became his armor. He also developed a stern look on his otherwise friendly and happy face. I felt Peter's pain and encouraged him to share his angers and frustrations with me. I frequently told him that some day he would meet a good woman who could appreciate his tender and sensitive personality.

Peter did well in school, but around the age of twelve his grades began to drop. I expressed disappointment in his performance. Nevertheless, his grades continued to drop a little each time he brought home a report card.

Adolescent Abroad

After one of our talks about school, life, and career, Peter realized that one reason he had begun to goof off in school was that he didn't want to be a "mama's boy" anymore. I was willing to accept that explanation, and from that day we had an unspoken pact. Peter was free to rebel, and I would be there to understand and support whatever he did. His parent-teacher conferences became more interesting. Previously, Peter and I would meet with his home room teacher only, but now all his teachers came to the meetings. They insisted that Peter could do much better in school than his grades showed. I smiled and politely agreed. However, I let them know that his grades would not improve until he was ready.

About the sane time Peter became interested in sex. One day when I came home from work, I was surprised to find the walls of his room covered with Playboy centerfolds that he had found in the community trash. I paused, then chose to ask him which he liked the best. He pointed out two that were his favorites. During the next few weeks Peter's friends made trips to our house more often than usual. They were all very interested in Peter's new photo gallery. After a couple of months I noticed that Peter had replaced the centerfolds with Star Wars pictures. I asked him what prompted him to redecorate his room. He said he was bored with the centerfolds. Shortly thereafter Peter showed me a porno magazine he had borrowed from a friend. The pictures were quite explicit. I was taken aback, but recovered quickly and tried to discuss the pictures in a matter-of-fact fashion. These events seemed to have satisfied Peter's immediate interest in sex.

Introducing Peter

Peter received an award for being "The Class Friendliest Boy" when he graduated from Junior High. That award was very appropriate, and I was proud of him. At school he was popular among fellow students, a leader in his peer group, and always courteous to his teachers. At home he was reading and discussing world issues with the enthusiasm and maturity of a college student, showing that he was learning in spite of his grades.

Peter always had an innocent and respectful interest in girls. He felt very comfortable around them and had many female friends. Those he fell in love with he put on a pedestal, but because he was very shy he never dated. In his mid-teens Peter began daydreaming about how wonderful it would be, some day, to have an intimate relationship with a woman and to be married. Money, career, and material goods would be meaningless if they weren't shared with someone he loved and adored. I was surprised he felt so strongly about marriage – my relationship with his father had been unsuccessful, and several of his friends came from broken homes. He thought it was because of the familial closeness he felt between he, Nila, and myself. Naturally, he would want to extend the love and respect he felt for the two most important people in his life to a spouse.

As the end of Peter's high school years approached, we spent much time discussing what the next chapter in his life should be. The summer prior to his senior year, he, Nila and I spent eight weeks in Scandinavia. Peter enjoyed that trip very much so we considered study abroad for one year in Denmark. Peter enjoyed learning about foreign countries, and had traveled to Asia as a cultural exchange during high school. Living outside the US, therefore, was not a surprising decision for Peter to make. He decided to spend a year studying at an international school in Copenhagen.

During Peter's final year of high school we prepared ourselves for the approaching separation. The last few months before he left, he began to pull away from Nila and me. We talked about it, and used analogies about separation that we knew from the animal world. For example, bear cubs learning to fend for themselves when the mother bear left them on their own. Although this was not an exact analogy of our situation, it helped to deal with the pending separation.

The day arrived for Peter to leave for Europe. His two close friends, Sam and Juan, Nila and myself were at the airport to see him off. He was pale and wore sunglasses. He had not slept well for several nights. His friends cracked a few jokes, and we laughed awkwardly. Peter and I held hands, but didn't say much to each other. His friends left shortly before Peter departed. Nila and I were holding on to him for a few more precious moments. He took his sunglasses off and looked into my eyes when we said goodbye. We both cried, but tried hard to be brave. While walking onto the plane, Peter turned around and waved to us. He was wearing his sunglasses again.

International phone calls were expensive, so we did not talk much during Peter's year in Denmark. As a result I received many letters in which he shared his feelings about growing up, and being away from home. We communicated with each other about how it felt to be apart from someone we loved so much.

Introducing Peter

Peter's letters expressed his dreams, frustrations, and fears as clearly as when we walked side by side.

Soon after Peter left his first letter arrived. I picked up the little blue envelope from the mailbox. I was so excited. The first thing I noticed was that the letter was addressed to Mom. My name was not on the envelope, just "Mom" and the address. I initially thought it must be unacceptable to send letters addressed to "Mom." But all Peter's letters were addressed that way. I later asked Peter why he didn't use my name. He proudly answered: "You are my Mom, not just a person with a name." I cherished that explanation.

– Marie Salten

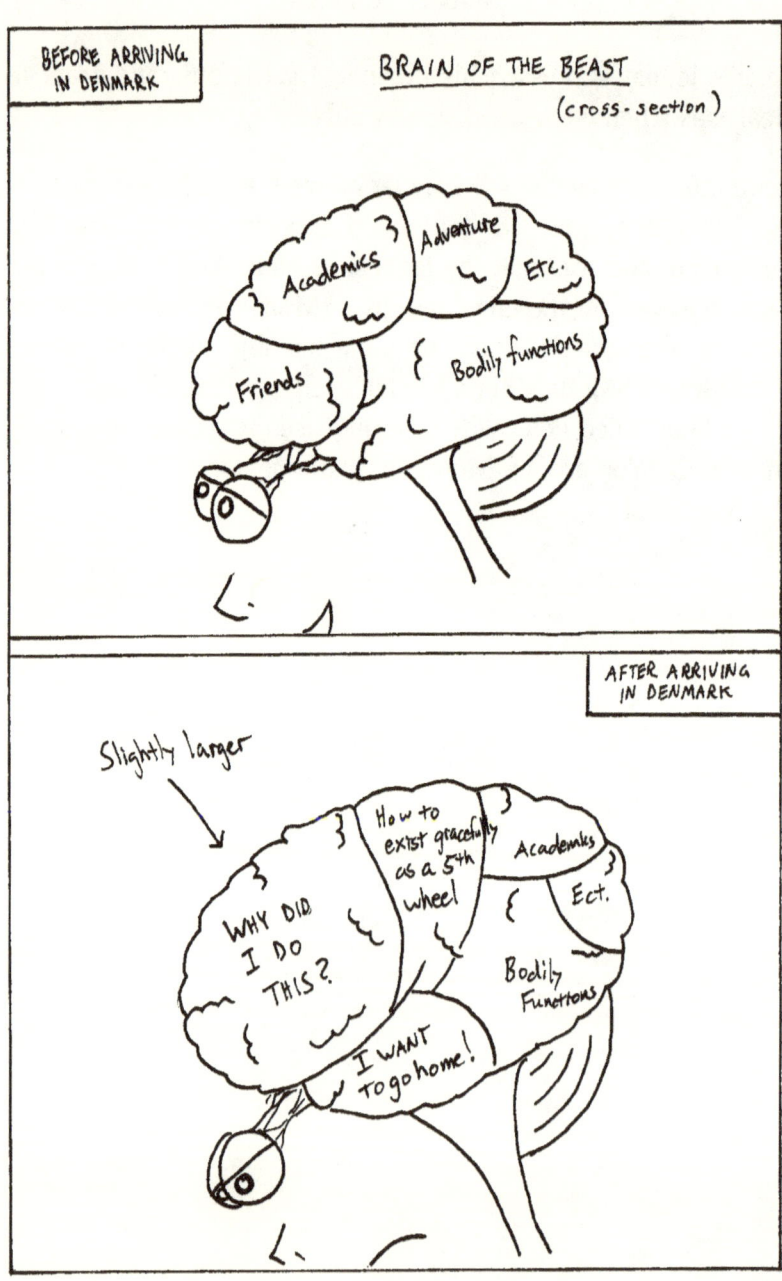

Section I. Getting Settled

This section includes six letters written during August and September. Peter explains how difficult it was to move away from home, enroll in a new school, and learn to survive in a foreign country. He experienced intense feelings of loneliness and emptiness. Though Peter gained a greater appreciation of his childhood years, he constructed a sentimental and unrealistic picture of the good times back home.

Letter 1 – Homesick

Before Peter arrived at his final destination in Copenhagen he visited my brother and his family in southern Sweden. He knew the family well. We had visited them during summer vacations, and they had travel to the US during winter. The family consisted of my brother, Valdemar, his wife, Eva, and their two children, Svend and Susan. Svend is one year younger than Peter, and Susan is three years younger. The family spoke English very well. It was comforting for me to know that they would pick Peter up at the airport and help him get settled in Denmark.

When Peter arrived, Valdemar and Eva were between jobs and the family was enjoying free time. In Sweden the welfare system pays ample unemployment wages, and the high standard of living there, even for unemployed people, was mind-boggling to Peter who recognized how I frugal I had to be even though I had a full-time job. Nevertheless, Peter felt a strong need to defend the U.S. socio-economic system and became very skeptical of Western European politics. In his first letter he expresses this skepticism.

August 7

Dear Mom.

I MISS YOU!!!!!

Whew! I had to get that out of my system. Well, I have been here for about four days now. Gosh, you wouldn't believe how horrible I felt when I got here. I felt like I had all my insides taken out of me, I was totally empty. As you could probably hear on the phone, I knew I missed you more than I ever have before. I even cried myself to sleep that night. Well, not really cried, more like sobbed. I finally woke up 18 hours later!! Don't ask me how, since my bed has to be the worst bed to sleep on in all of Sweden.

I sure miss waking up to ♬ GOOD MORNING....GOOD MORNING!! ♬ Tra la la bum dum tra la la bum ♬! Remember how much I hated when you woke me up singing that tune? Now I miss it so much!!!

Golf is the new "in" sport here in Sweden. First, it was soccer, then it was tennis, and now it is golf!!! Sounds like these Swedes are getting wimpy, eh! I feel like I am in an entire country of spoiled snobs. And you thought the Americans were bad with their "instant gratification" bit. You ain't seen nothing yet. They have a lot more crime too than I realized!! You would love it out here, though, the socialist that you are. People without a job are living better than we are! I haven't changed much yet! I'm still picking on the Commies. Where was I, oh yes, golf. Yes, the whole family out here is enrolled in golf classes, and I practice with them. See, out here you need to be certified to play golf!! Guess what we do in our spare time? We play mini-golf! It is fun, but I lose all the time. They have had more practice than I, and there mini-golf courses do not have any little buildings like ours.

I guess you will have a dog by the time you return my letter, so you better send a picture of it. I miss you so much!!!!

Letter 1 – Homesick

Love you, Peter

P.S. I haven't heard "Highwayman" since I got here!!!

AAAAARRRRGGGG!!!!

Peter liked country music, and "Highwayman" was one of his favorite songs. It became popular in the late 1980s, when Peter's favorite country singers, Willie Nelson, Waylon Jennings, Kris Kristoffersen, and Johnny Cash, released their version of the song. The song is about the reincarnation of spirit in four men who die under various circumstances. Peter liked the stories and felt that they had a special meaning or message to him.

After Peter left, our house was very quiet. Nila wanted a dog to keep us company and liven up the house like Peter used to do. We went to the animal shelter to find a "substitute" for Peter. We chose a small black puppy who followed us around wherever we went. We called her Shadow.

Letter 2 – My New Pad

While in school in Denmark, Peter stayed with a close friend of mine, Anja, whom I met during my college years in Copenhagen. She and I kept in touch, and I often met with her when I visited Denmark.

Anja had never married or been around children, so I realized that housing a lively teenager like Peter would be a big undertaking. However, when Peter and I visited Copenhagen the year before he moved, Anja offered to house Peter. I felt a sense of comfort knowing Peter would live with Anja.

Anja lived in a big house located just outside Copenhagen. It consisted of three apartments and a small room in the basement where Peter stayed. He was able to use the kitchen and the phone located upstairs in Anja's apartment. The remaining apartments were occupied by two Danish women. In the following letter Peter describes his arrival at Anja's house.

August 14

Dear Mom.

How are you? Fine I hope. Me, I miss all of you so much.

I am in Denmark now. Oh, that reminds me, I better put the date in the corner of the letter. Today, I took care of all the bank stuff and the bus pass. Tomorrow, I will sign up for health care and get my ten digit ID number. I have learned you can't do anything without the ID number. I even had trouble in the bank because I didn't have it! I am also going to the school. I'll call first and ask about a financial aid form. Then, I will explore and practice the bus routes. Gosh, just writing to you brings tears to my eyes.

When I came here Anja and I had to leave right away to take care of some business, but she said to me: "Oh Peter, you already got a letter." I was so excited, then she said: "But you can't read it until you get back." Now I see why, the letter was from you of course, and I cried through the whole letter. Gosh, it is so hard crying out here because I have no one to comfort me. Oh well, I better quit acting like a baby. Anyway, I am doing a lot of crying. I hope all the fun I am suppose to have starts soon or it is gonna be a long year.

Get this, a couple of days after writing my first letter to you, I got a piece of iron lodged in my eye!! RELAX, RELAX, it's not as bad as it sounds, but it sure hurt like hell!!! Anyhow, the damn thing was stuck in my eye, I couldn't get it out. So I had to go to the hospital and have some minor, and I mean minor, surgery done on my left eye. First, they put this junk in my eye so it went numb, then, they stuck my head in a machine that kept it still, and they shined a light in my eye so that I couldn't see. I didn't see what kind of tools they used (because I didn't want to know), but they finally dug it out. You know these people who look real stupid because they have a big white patch on their eye? Well, I was one of them for a couple of days. Oh well, I always wanted to be a pirate.

I'm sorry that so much of this letter is bad news, but if you measured my thoughts by the number of pages I write, I would

Letter 2 – My New Pad

have to write ten saying "I love you" another ten saying "I miss you" and then this with the bad news. But all of that would get repetitive.

I love you so much!! I miss you too, hope to see you soon.

Love Peter

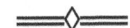

It took Peter 20 minutes to travel from Anja's house to the center of Copenhagen where his school was located. The school was a private international institution, where all lectures were held in English. It provided education mainly for children of diplomats, ambassadors, and foreign professionals working in Denmark, as well as children of Danish parents seeking a private education in English.

Because both Peter's father and I were Danish citizens when he was born, Peter automatically became a Danish citizen. Upon arriving in Denmark he was, therefore, able to apply for health care coverage and educational aid.

Letter 3 – Starting School

In Denmark the basic unit of currency is the Kroner, which is divided into one hundred Ore. During Peter's stay in Denmark, one U.S. dollar could buy approximately six Danish kroner. Peter was acquainted with the monetary conversion from previous trips to Denmark and had little difficultly adjusting.

Understanding the public transportation system, however, could be challenging. Peter made sure he learned the bus system quickly so he could find his way around Copenhagen and get to school on time.

August 19

Dear Mom.

Wow, this is the third letter I'm writing you, and I haven't even finished writing my friends yet. I miss you guys terribly, but I am starting to feel better though, since I started school yesterday. I made three friends too. I didn't feel nervous at all. I guess it's gonna be tough to scare me now, compared to the fear I felt about leaving home. A lot of the students here are part Danish like me. Two of my friends are Danish-American. Sean is from New York, Jess is from Chicago, and the third is of Slovakian-Danish mix; his name is Niels. His dad owns a Slovakian restaurant here. So next Friday after school we are all going there for free dinner. They seem like a good bunch of guys, and we're all new to the school. I'm sure I'll be making a lot more friends since everyone seems pretty nice. I might have a problem with one southern European guy who has been giving me dirty looks. He is kinda big, almost as tall as me, but I'm pretty sure I can kick his ass! Don't worry, I am not gonna start anything with him, I'm smart. They are making me take English, Danish, German, higher Math, higher Physics, and Social Anthropology, so I can't take P.E. The Danish teacher is a "fox!" and she seems to like me already. The German teacher is an American student teacher. She's real sweet, and pretty young, she seems to like me too.

Oh yeah, you know how Nila collects cans to sell. Well, I've started collecting bottles. I get one Danish kroner per bottle. My friends at school think it is funny, but they know I'm pinching pennies, so they help me out. Nila should crush all the cans so she can fit more cans into a bag, like we used to do at our grandparents house. This way she won't feel like she is getting so little money for so much work.

Hey, that's too bad about the Goodwill store being robbed. Was it my store or the main store? Mom, could you give me the address to my store, I didn't write it in my book.

Thanks for cutting out the last strips of "Bloom County". I'm glad I got to see how it ended. It was sad though, especially Sunday's strip. God, it even made me cry, I felt like Opus and I were the same person; both leaving everything behind. Sheesh! I'm getting to be too sensitive. I'm crying all the time out here it seems.

Right before my first day of school, I got your letter that said you and Nila cry sometimes because you miss me. That made

Letter 3 – Starting School

me feel good, like you guys were there to wish me luck on my first day or something. I cried.

Anja is real good to me. We usually have coffee in the morning and talk about controversial topics. I love doing that you know. Sometimes she just answers my questions about Denmark. Tonight she is cooking me dinner, chicken and rice. God, I miss that dish. I am glad to eat a cooked meal that I didn't make. I'm an awful cook. Don't worry, she first made me sweep the sidewalk, which I was more than happy to do. They have to sweep their sidewalks out here. Isn't that weird?!!

Oh yeah, I wonder if you could get me some acid-washed jeans. I wear size 33 by 33. They are so expensive out here, and they have a difficult way of sizing. I know you told me to get some at the store before I left. But I was too much of a hard-head. What else can I say but "Peter, you're such an asshole!" That was from the movie "Arthur" only the name has been changes (to protect the innocent).

Thanks for giving me your credit card number to call the U.S. But to tell you the truth, I'm afraid to. See, night time is when we get the best rate here. But it's also when I get homesick, and I don't want to call up and start crying. So I'll have to stick to letters.

The other night Anja wasn't home, so I watched a video, and it just wasn't the same without the popcorn, ice cream, sodas, and popcorn farts. I got so homesick "I thought I was gonna die." I was so sad, even my heart started hurting. I don't think I've ever been that sad in my life!! Sorry, I didn't mean to make you worry or anything, I just want you to know how much I miss you.

Did I tell you I finally shaved? Well, I hate it! Anja didn't like my beard at all, so I said "what the hell." I was curious to see what I looked like under it anyway. But I hate it, so now I'm gonna grow it back.

Anja wanted to know how much a hot air popcorn popper costs, a new one, not one from the goodwill store. Could you check on that please.

Oh yeah, one more thing, I know you want to know if we're eight or nine hours ahead of you, but nobody I talked to knows. Oh well, if it helps, its 8:30 PM out here right now, ha' ha! I miss you so much, but don't worry, I should get better now that school started. Say "Hi" to my friends if you see them. I love you so much. Bye!!!

Love, Peter

It was important for Peter to communicate with his friends back home, and they were eager to learn about his adventures in Europe. Although overseas calls were expensive, I gave Peter my phone card number, and trusted that he would not abuse it.

Since Peter's departure, our house had been quiet and dinners unexciting. Peter used to make them very exciting. He, Nila, and I would talk about sociological, psychological, and political issues. Peter and I rarely agreed, and we each eagerly tried to convince the other that our own opinions

Letter 3 – Starting School

were best. He enjoyed discussing such issues with Anja as well, and she enjoyed it too. When she and I were in college together, we spent many hours trying to "fix' the world.

We also discussed movies during dinner; the ones we had seen and the ones we wanted to see. We were the last family among Peter's friends to have a VCR. Peter, Nila, and I really celebrated when we finally picked one out. We rarely watch television, but every other Saturday evening we rented a movie. The three of us took turns choosing what movie to watch. We had popcorn, ice cream, and soft drinks. Each of us had certain chores to prepare for the occasion. For example, Peter made popcorn and was responsible for rewinding the movies before we returned them to the store. Nila served soft drinks and ice cream. She also kept track of whose turn it was to choose a movie. She kept her schedule on the refrigerator. It was a big event. When the movie finished, we enjoyed discussing it and learning how we each interpreted it.

Newspaper cartoons were another topic of discussion. Peter's favorite cartoon was "Bloom County." The series stopped shortly after he went to Denmark, and I had promised to send him the last cartoons, so he could find out how it ended.

I also promised to send Peter the address to the local Goodwill store where he worked during the summer before going to Denmark. He had enjoyed working there, and wanted to express his sympathy to the boss and former co-workers when he learned that the store had been robbed.

Adolescent Abroad

Peter never worked during the school year. I wanted him to enjoy his youth, and his job was to get good grades in school. In Western Europe it is highly unusual that students work during the school year. They, typically, have three to five hours homework daily, and working instead of doing schoolwork is frowned upon by European parents. Being European, I agreed with that view.

Letter 4 – A Cute Girl

Peter loved to learn and spent much time reading the encyclopedia and some of my college text books. His favorite was my biology book. He became an honor student throughout high school without putting much time and effort into homework. In Denmark, however, he quickly discovered that his academic preparation was weak compared to the other students. This was partly the result of significant differences in educational standards between European schools and most American schools. The problem was compounded by Peter's preoccupation with learning how to get along on his own in a foreign country.

Peter was very unhappy about his inferior academic standing in Denmark, and felt very lowly compared to his peers at the new school. He developed feelings of inferiority and hopelessness which lingered throughout his stay in Denmark.

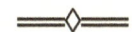

September 3

Dear Mom.

Hello again from Denmark. Well first of all, thanks for all the wonderful postcards. I was also glad to hear how my friends are doing in your letter. I wish they would write me though. It is getting much easier to read your letters now that school has started and I'm not so lonely. Before when I read about something I missed, I used to cry, but now I giggle or laugh to myself when I remember all the great times. School is so difficult out here; the homework is ridiculous, about four to five hours a night. So naturally, I do half that, since I start feeling my brain is telling me to stop before it explodes. I talked to the counselor about it. She said there are other students in the same situation as me. They tend to have a little trouble with the work load, because of the difference in school systems, loneliness, and the stress of living on their own. It made sense to me since I spend about half my day thinking about home (probably more). So tomorrow we are going to work out an easier schedule, but I have mixed feelings about it. On one hand I feel relieved, but on the other hand, I feel like I can't handle it because I'm stupid. There is a girl in my class from India named Isha. We have been talking during our free periods, and she seemed very mature, sophisticated, and interesting to talk to. Plus she's not too bad looking and she seems to have an interest in me. A few days later I asked her what year she is. I assumed she was in 12th or 13th, but noooooo, she's in 10th grade, AAAAAAARR-RRRGGGG!!!! Nila's age for Pete's sake! I figured this must be because of all those bad religious jokes I used to tell; now God is trying to get back at me. Well, it is not gonna work, cause I am thinking about sticking with her.

Dad's father is visiting in Denmark, so I met him today. We walked around in Copenhagen, and he introduced me to some of my relatives on that side of the family. Then we called Dad. He was really happy to hear from me, and I was happy to talk to him. But then I got homesick again, and I started to think about you and Nila. That's why I'm writing you. The only people I haven't written to are Shane, Karen, and ....ANN. I will write Ann, even though she treated me lousy. I still miss her, a lot! I

Letter 4 – A Cute Girl

know, you are probably going, "damn Peter, give it up, will ya!" But I'm stubborn.

Well, it sure was nice hearing your voice when I called. When I call next time I hope Nila is there too, and I want to talk to the dog, make him bark or something. Now that you only have Nila in school over there, you are probably only getting one newsletter instead of two. So to ease your suffering I'll send our school newsletter to you.

I hope to hear from you soon. I LOVE YOU.

Love Peter "Beast"

P.S. YIKES, I forgot to tell you that Lana is coming to visit in January. She found a deal where she could fly round trip for $500. Isn't that great!!! I can't wait. Love you Peter.

I had always felt close to Peter's friends. They often came to our house to play or talk. When Peter left for Denmark, his friends still called our house and stopped by to check on me. Lana, a friend of Peter's since grammar school, would be able to visit him over the Christmas break. Peter was very pleased to be receiving company from home, especially around the holidays.

Ann, on the other hand, was a young woman Peter met and fell in love with during his senior year of high school. She had an off-and-on boyfriend and never reciprocated Peter's love. She stood him up a couple of times just prior to his move to Denmark. Peter was hurt, but still wanted to keep in touch with her during his year overseas. Holding on to all the ties back home became a priority for Peter; and receiving letters from old friends kept his spirit high.

Peter's paternal grandfather took the opportunity to visit Peter while on a trip Copenhagen. He and his wife were both from Denmark and had immigrated to the States when Peter's father was a child. Peter was their first grandchild, and they adored him. We lived close to them while Peter was young and visited often. When Peter got older he liked to vacation at their house during summers. In Denmark Peter met his grandfather's family and friends and acquired a better understanding of his Danish heritage.

In appearance Peter fits the Viking stereotype. He is tall and robust, has fair skin and blond curly hair. His disposition is like that of a modern Dane, outgoing and witty. His friends quickly gave him the nickname "Beast" at his new school. He liked that name, it made him feel big and powerful.

Letter 5 – Getting Drafted

While Peter's grandfather was in Denmark, he persuaded Peter to call his father back in the States. It had been a long time since Peter talked to his father, who had not been part of either Peter or Nila's lives for several years. This was very painful for Peter, and he tried time and again to get his father's attention, but to no avail. This time their conversation was good, and his father promised to write Peter. His father had also lived in Denmark for a short time during his teenage years. They now had something in common, and Peter felt their relationship could be rekindled through sharing their similar experience.

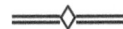

September 5

Dear Mom.

Thanks Mom for the letter and the advice. I have finally finished writing everyone at least once. It pays off too, I get a letter almost every day. I think that's what keeps me going sometimes. Every day I rush home from school to see if I got a letter. Last Monday I got your letter and a very nice letter from Pia. Then today, I got one from Dad. He told me about his experience when he came out here and stuff. It is nice to know that he can still help me out.

I am on a bit of a downer now. Just when things were starting to get good. I don't know where to begin with my problems, sheesh. O.K., first of all, I can feel that the friends I have made will probably not be my friends in the next few weeks to come.

Adolescent Abroad

Nearly all of them have girlfriends now, and they have problems with their girlfriends. Me, I'm so busy trying to get my stuff together that the thought of a girlfriend hardly crosses my mind. I know that sounds unbelievable. Besides there is not a big selection here, and most of them are taken already. And forget about the girls outside school, the people in the city are so unfriendly! I'm just glad they aren't allowed to have guns.

Next, I got drafted into the Danish army. Anja and I are in the middle of straightening that out now. God, then she jumped all over my case today for a bunch of things I forgot to do, like cleaning up. My first reaction was: "darn, lighten up will you," but once I thought about it, she was right. I'm forgetting things, that I should easily remember. The same thing happens in school, especially in math. It's like I had a lobotomy or something. I've forgotten even basic math. The counselor is thinking about moving me to a lower level, but that stuff I've had before. I've already gotten rid of English and German, and I'm taking history instead. Anyway, I'm starting to feel like a loser. I don't even know what kind of career I want. Engineering is out, because of my lousy math abilities. This is all scaring me. I used to feel in complete (or nearly complete) control of myself. Now I feel like a lost, loser, idiot. I know you told me this is MY year, but I feel I am wasting it.

I am very proud of Nila though and her interest in modeling. How is she doing in school? I can't wait to see her and Lana this Christmas. I've only been here for a month, and it feels like a year. Sorry this letter wasn't a happy letter. I know you want me to have lots of fun. Oh well, at least I'll stick it out. I hope things are better back home. I miss you lots.

Letter 5 – Getting Drafted

Love Peter

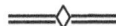

I realized Peter would have difficulties adapting to his new life in Denmark, but I had not foreseen his academic problems. He had been very confident and successful in high school. I often wanted to call him after receiving one of his unhappy letters, yet I recognized that he needed to deal with his problems on his own.

When Peter was unhappy he complained about almost everything. In this letter he expressed discontent with the Danish people. I believe his feelings were unjust. Danes are very peaceful and scorn handguns, but they do have an army. Because Peter was a Danish citizen, he was drafted. However he was exempted once he let the draft board know that he was in Denmark as a student for only one year.

Luckily Peter received frequent letters throughout his stay in Denmark. They helped him through his unhappy periods. Peter had just received a letter from Pia. She had been in love with Peter throughout high school, and asked him to their senior prom. Peter's feelings toward her were like those for a sister. He was, therefore, happy when he later learned through a friend that she had a boyfriend.

Peter was proud of his little sister who was pursuing a modeling career. Her success became more important to him since he perceived himself as a failure. He felt that at least I could be proud of one of them.

Letter 6 – New Friends

In this letter Peter reminded me about the eye injury he suffered while visiting my brother Valdemar and his family in Sweden. After the incident, Eva took Peter to the emergency room for treatment. Fortunately, he did not have any permanent damage from the injury.

It seemed so long since the accident had happened, and since Peter left home. Shadow, the small dog Nila and I acquired shortly after Peter left, was already getting big. We took pictures of her and sent them to Peter. He liked the way she looked, and when he came back home he really bonded with her.

Peter had always loved animals. Unfortunately, we did not have pets while he was growing up. I personally felt that caring for two children as a single parent was plenty of work.

September 16

Dear Mom.

Thank you so much for the picture of your new dog "Shadow." He's cute. By the way, is it a boy or a girl? I wish I could pet him. I'll bet he brings lots of life into the house, so hopefully, it isn't so silent at dinner anymore. Of course he can't get into those good discussions with you, that I did. Anja's cat hates me. I wish Shadow could come over here and eat it.

Adolescent Abroad

O.K., since you missed out on the story about my eye, here it goes. It happened while I was in Sweden. Svend and I were riding the bikes right next to a construction site, and all of a sudden TWEEK, I fell something nail my eye. You know me, I held in the scream, and just closed my left eye while water was pouring out of it. I managed to keep it hidden till we got home. I hurried into the bathroom and tried to dig it out. It looked like it would be easy to take it out, but after hundreds of attempts, I realized I needed help. I was thinking: "Great, this is just what I need, to go through a year in Europe without an eye. I can just forget about getting laid now." Eva took me to the hospital, and after waiting for an hour or so they finally started to operate on it. Apparently, they did not think it was as serious as I did. Remember how I always freaked when they showed eye surgery on TV? Well, you can imagine how I was feeling. Then they poured this stuff in my eye that made it numb, and then shined the light right into my pupil so I wouldn't see anything. My other eye was covered and my head was in a vise so I wouldn't move. From then on, all I heard was the clanging of metal instruments they were using to remove the object from my eye. I could feel my eye being forced into strange shapes from the nerves inside my eye. Finally, it was over. They poured some goop in my eye, that was suppose to make it heal fast, and then they put an eye patch on my eye. I had to keep my eye closed while it was healing, so I slept about 30 out of 48 hours. The object was a steel splinter. It was very small, but felt huge. Needless to say, I'm over my pirate stage now.

Ha! I was cracking up when you told me why Nila liked the picture you sent of her. I'm keeping it hidden, though, so none of my friends see it. She is probably having a lot of fun this year

Letter 6 – New Friends

now that I'm not around to babysit her. Of course my friends promised they would look out for her while I was gone. She just needs to be strong and take things as they come, not freak out like I did. Sometimes you just have to say screw it, it is not my problem. And as for you Mom, shame on you for ditching school. At least you told me the truth and it was an accident. Remember I used to ditch and tell you about it, so I guess it's your turn now.

Thanks for the address to the Goodwill store. Anja says if you get a popcorn popper, she insists on paying for it.

I hear football season started, so please let me know how my favorite teams are doing. The Vikings, of course, the Rams and the Raiders.

Oh yeah, and since you were wondering about my weekends. Don't worry, they are great. It's when I'm in school that I have a hard time, because I feel like I'm so much less than the other students.

You can probably tell by my tone in this letter that I am in much better spirits than I was in my last letter. It's because I wrote my last letter during the week. Last night my friends and I went out and messed around. We were out till about 2:00 AM. We are a big group of friends, about 20 people. But within the group there are a few of us who are a bit closer. See, the rest are younger, and they are so worried about impressing the rest of us, and they are trying to be perfect. I was with the small group last night. We are more down to earth and have deeper concerns than the others. The group is:

JESS – He's a real fun guy, pretty wild and funny when he gets drunk

NELLA – Jess' girlfriend sort of. She is real nice. We stay over at her house a lot, since her basement has six beds to sleep on.

JANE – She is a cute girl, but a little nuts. I think she is confused since she has lived in three countries for about the same length of time. Denmark, U.S.A., and the Middle East.

SEAN – He is the most interesting of them. He and I are alike in a lot of ways. We both switch on and off, feeling like a fifth wheel in the group. He is the only one I've really had a good, and I mean good, talk with. The kind you and I used to have. He and I have a hard time getting close to anyone. I guess its because we have lives in the States that we don't want to let go of. What is weird is, I think he can sense the same things about me.

Anyway, all of us are a lot alike in that we are all Danish-American students and we spend a lot of time being homesick. But none of them could replace my old friends, whom I miss so much. You don't know what you got until you see it from a distance. Gosh! I love those guys, and I love you so much. I better go now, and I hope to hear from you again soon. Bye, bye, or as they say here, Hi! Hi!

Love Peter

P.S. I am starting to get fat from too much bread and beer. Should I join a gym?

Letter 6 – New Friends

Peter referred to having occasionally ditched high school. I never scolded him about misbehavior; we would discuss his actions and consider potential consequences. By addressing his conduct in this manner, the excitement of misbehaving disappeared and Peter turned out to be a very well behaved young man.

I wanted to be close to my children and enjoyed seeing them unfold. I also wanted them to know me too, not just as their mother, but as a person and a friend. Consequently, we spent much time sharing our thoughts and feelings, and loved each other unconditionally. When Peter mentioned in his letter that he cracked up because Nila "liked the picture you sent of her," it exemplified the appreciation he had for her. In the picture she was wearing shorts and a bikini top while holding Shadow in such a way that she showed a little cleavage. Being a budding adolescent, she was proud of her new curves, and Peter was able to appreciate her pride.

To maintain closeness in our family, much time was devoted to communication and just 'hanging out" with each other. I often sat up to the wee hours of the night talking with Peter. He had strong emotions, an inquisitive mind, and a great need to talk. When he was unhappy, he would bounce his feelings off me. Then go on his merry way, feeling like he had come to a new understanding of himself and the world around him.

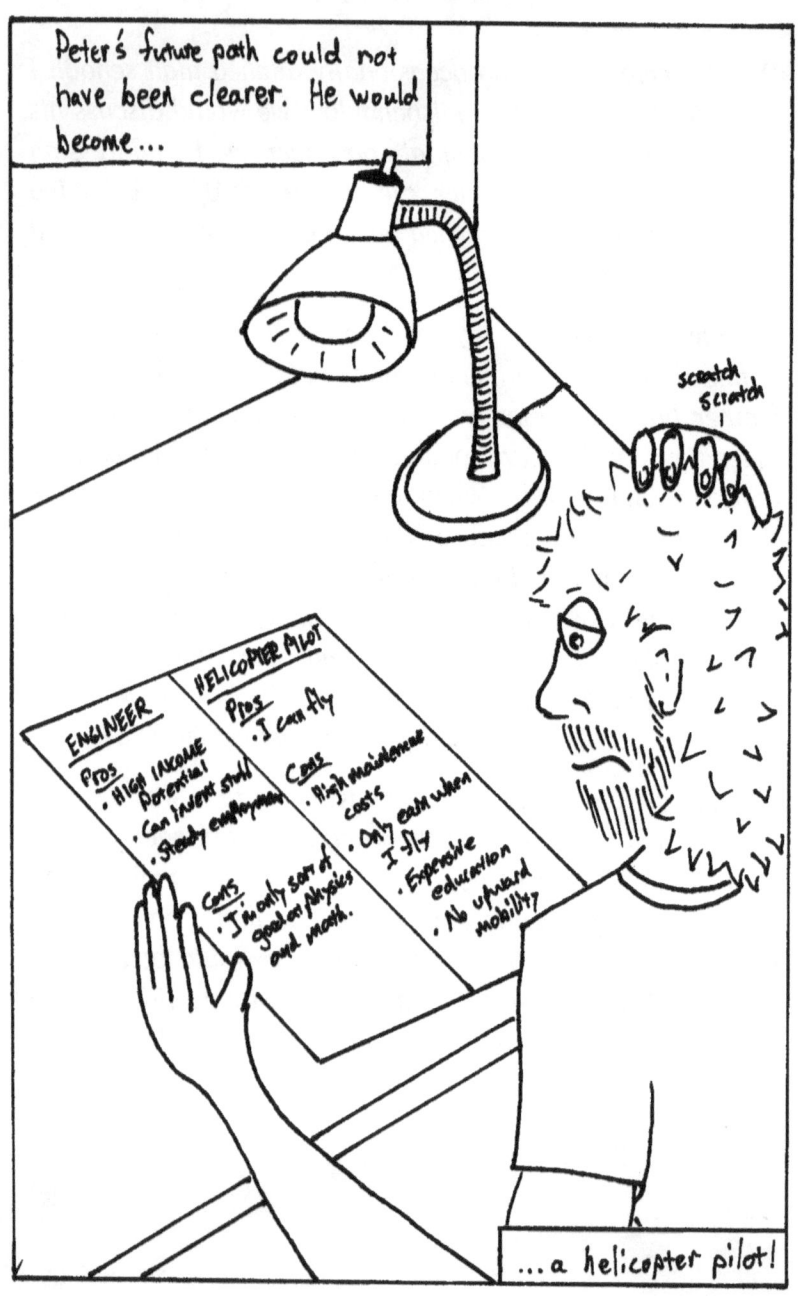

Section II. Choosing a Career

During the fall months Peter wrote seven letters in which he elaborated on his confusion about choosing a suitable career. He was overwhelmed by the amount of information he received from universities and the cost of an education. As a result he felt hopeless about the future.

On a lighter note, Peter had his first sexual encounter during this period. He also made an exciting trip to Southern Europe. These events temporarily boosted his spirits and he eagerly shared them in his letters.

Letter 7 – Letters from Friends

It had been almost 20 years since I immigrated to the U.S., and like many expatriates, I had developed a sentimental attitude toward Denmark. I grew up in a small farming community where everyone knew everyone else. People rarely moved into or out of our town, and greetings came with a friendly smile. I often conveyed these happy memories to Peter, but he had seen a different Denmark during our visits. This was partly because we spent much time in big cities, such as Copenhagen. But the countryside still seems quaint and peaceful. Living in suburban Copenhagen, Peter experienced Denmark differently than I had during my childhood.

Peter's political views might also have colored his perception of Denmark. He was very conservative, and Denmark is very liberal. Peter valued individualism, and took issues with the Danish political system and its collectivism.

In my letters to Peter I described my own experiences of alienation and loneliness when I first came to the United States. This helped him understand his feelings and emotions about living in a foreign country.

September 27

Dear Mom.

Adolescent Abroad

This is weird, I was at school today and some of my friends asked me to the movies, but I said "nope." I sensed that I had finally received a letter after about a week and a half of no letters. So when I got home, there was a stack of letters for me. Two from Japan and seven from all you guys at home. I was so happy. Now I can answer all your questions and tell you how things are going.

First of all, I am better now. I have completely accepted my situation, and I have learned that I may as well enjoy it. I just said to myself: "Hey self, screw it, you are here and there is nothing that can change that; and you know, that even if you could get back to the States, you wouldn't, because then you would really have failed yourself."

The classes are still hard, but I am slowly, I mean slowly, improving. I am starting to look for colleges now. I still think I should trash the engineering idea. I don't think I will enjoy doing math and physics behind a desk for the rest of my life. So now, being a helicopter pilot is my goal, again! I could learn it in the army for free, but I promised you I'd go to college, plus you know how I am about taking orders. So now I have to figure out how to learn it in college... I don't know, I hope you will give me some input on this stuff. College will be here before I know it and I haven't the slightest idea about what to do.

By the way, in one of your letters you wrote "therapist," and I thought you wrote "the rapist," remember, you can only divide a word like that between syllables ther-a-pist, see.

Letter 7 – Letters from Friends

Well, here is the Danish news. First today, this morning when I went to meet some friends at Vesterport train station, I was ushered away by the police because of a bomb that they were diffusing inside. Also I realized that I see about two car-chases each weekend. You know, the kind in the movies with lots of speeding police cars and undercover cars. Pretty exciting. I thought this was strange, so I asked a Danish friend of mine: "what the hell is going on?" He told me: "Peter, didn't you know that Copenhagen has the highest crime rate in Europe." I almost said: "that is not what my Mommy said." Of course, most of the crime is non-violent or at least non-lethal. Things have changed a bit, haven't they MOM! Ha! Ha!

Oh yeah, I may as well clear up that I am not going to Portugal, only Spain, near Barcelona, a place called "Costa Brava." It is about a nine hour train ride to Portugal from where we will be staying in Spain, and I gotta really watch my money, because... get this, I turned in my financial aid form, and the secretary said: "Ok, if they accept it you'll probably get the money the quarter after your eighteenth birthday. FEBRUARY!!! I just about fainted. I said: "A hellova lot of good that will do me then." Dammit!! All she would say was: "Well, that's the way the system works!" I figured that I can probably make it till Christmas, but Santa Claus isn't delivering any presents from me that's for sure.

The other day Anja and I went to see "Indiana Jones III." She and I are getting along pretty well. She does get on my case every once in a while for not cleaning up. That is cool, I know I deserve it.

Adolescent Abroad

Grandpa is going back to the States tomorrow. It was nice seeing him. He showed me a lot of the places where his family lives, in case I get in trouble. I also visited your father. That was...well, you can guess how that went. He made some weird food for me, and I tried hard to act as if I liked it.

Oh, I better clear up another thing. I am not going for Isha, the girl from India anymore, however, we are very good friends. I don't really know if I am in love with any of these girls or if I ever would be. And what do I know about love anyway. Sam told me that Ann is getting fat and ugly, I am sorry to hear that. I just got the nicest, sweetest letter from her, it made me feel soooo good. How is this for a strange event, even though she was the last one of my friends that I wrote to (I was kind of bitter about being treated like dirt by her), she was one of the first of my friends to write me back.

Thank you so much for the new pictures of "Shadow." She sounds so cute. I could just picture her playing with your stuffed animals. I wish I could watch her grow and play with her. Make sure she is well behaved, though, and on special occasions give her some good meat instead of dog food, since she is part of the family too.

Thanks for all the letters, MOM. They help me out a lot. It sounds like you know exactly what I am going through out here.

Well, I grew my beard back. It's much nicer now. And my hair is starting to get real long in the back. When it is wet, it goes to the middle of my shoulder blades, so I am happy about that. By the time I return to the States, I should look like a real savage BEAST.

Letter 7 – Letters from Friends

By the way, what is it like at home now that everyone has the same political viewpoint? I can't imagine how weird that must be. Don't worry, I haven't turned into a Commie, so just wait till I get back. Also don't forget to keep me posted on my favorite football teams.

I remember you were wondering about my weekends. Well, they are just perfect. I party hard every weekend. People love having me at their parties, because I totally liven them up. Also I can drink more than almost everyone without throwing up or waking up with a hang-over. Guess who I inherited that from?

Mom I love you to pieces, Nila too, and I miss you. Well, it is an hour past my bedtime, as you can probably tell by all the mistakes in the letter. I love you.

Love Peter

P.S. Because of daylight savings time we are now only eight hours ahead of you.

P.S. Say Hi to all my friends. Luv Ya!

Peter studied Japanese and became president of the Asian Studies Club at his school. He also had the privilege of being a cultural exchange student, and spent two weeks with a family in Japan. He truly enjoyed the country and the family he stayed with. He kept in close contact with them and was happy to find two letters from them one day after school.

Fortunately Peter received many letters in Denmark. He is a people person, and enjoys corresponding with family and friends. He had developed strong interpersonal and diplomatic skills by pushing every rule and regulation I set for him. He was not a compliant youngster; not disagreeable either, but wanted to be involved in the formation of every decision I made concerning him, and we compromised on each guideline I set. Thus, I felt that he had excellent skills to become a diplomat in the foreign services. He liked that idea, but had also been fascinated with helicopters and airplanes from an early age, and couldn't wait to fly them himself. In high school he took an IQ test on which he scored extremely high on the visual-spacial part; that fact reinforced his wish to fly aircraft. Every now and then he also talked about becoming an engineer or an architect.

I had hoped that my brother or my father could provide Peter with encouraging male guidance and helpful career advice. However, my brother moved to northern Sweden shortly after Peter arrived in Denmark, and it was not possible for Peter to visit him there on a regular basis. My father, on the other hand, lived by himself in a small town outside Copenhagen. By train and bus it could take up to two hours to arrive at his house. He rarely socialized. He enjoyed his house and stayed busy harvesting fruit and vegetables in his yard. He was also an excellent craftsman and always in the midst of remodeling. He spoke some English, but had become hard of hearing. It was difficult for him to hold a good conversation with Peter, who tended to talk fast and swallow parts of words. My father prepared food by mixing fruits and vegetables together in a large pot and boiling them with oats. This type of cooking was not Peter's favorite. My children had a curious interest in my father though. He visited us several times in the States when

Letter 7 – Letters from Friends

they were younger, and we visited him in Denmark. He was very different from any other human being they knew; they admired him, but also felt uneasy around him. Peter had just visited him but did not want to return without me present.

So Peter stayed in Copenhagen and socialized with his friends during free time. He liked Copenhagen, even though it was not as peaceful as I had told him. He never believed me in the first place, and now he could prove me wrong. He liked that.

In his humorous way Peter liked to point out to me when I was wrong. For example, when I pronounced a word incorrectly or used an improper word in a sentence. In my last letter to him I had divided the word "therapist" as we would in the Danish language. Dividing words and sentences is different in Danish than in American-English. Thus, Peter and I would every now and then misunderstand what we were trying to communicate to each other.

Letter 8 – Checking-out Universities

I was excited about prospect of Peter going to a university where he could learn to fly. The financial aspect of a university education did not worry me. My primary concern was to support Peter in whatever he wanted to do; loans could always be paid off later.

I also encouraged Peter to travel as much as possible during his stay in Europe. My parents had allowed me to travel outside of Denmark when I was young. I had many good memories from those trips, and I wanted Peter to have the same experience. Looking forward to trips, hopefully, would make time go faster for Peter and improve his spirits when he felt sad and lonely. In this letter Peter looks forward to his upcoming travels.

October 9

Dear Mom.

Hi! How are things at home? Pretty good out here. Yesterday, I spent ten hours doing a history report. Funny, everything seems so easy now that it is done. Today, we had representatives from 22 different U.S. colleges at our school. I was looking at the university at Hawaii. Surprisingly, it was the least expensive one; only about $10,500 per year for everything. I think that is incredibly expensive, but considered cheap by most of my classmates. However, that place does not have what I want, so they are not getting ten grand out of this kid. I saw a different college, though, that looks perfect for me. It is called "The

Florida Institute of Technology." It looks pretty good. First of all, it is warm. Second, there is a beach. And third, they have a real good aviation program. I couldn't believe it, they teach you how to fly right there in school. I was so excited! I asked the lady if they trained students to fly helicopters. She said they didn't, but a lot of students who want to fly helicopters, come to their school, because first, you have to be a qualified fixed wing pilot. That's not all, they also have a real good ocean study program (oceanography, marine biology, marine engineering, etc.). She's gonna send me some more information soon. I will also send you some pamphlets, in case you want to see what the school is all about.

I got your early birthday cards today. Thank you. I wish so bad I could see you for my birthday. It's gonna be so weird not to celebrate my 18th birthday with anyone from home. If you see Sam, tell him "Happy Birthday," too! His birthday is the 18th. I'm going to the bank tomorrow with the check you sent me. I'm gonna try not to spend too much money in Spain, because I could really use the money here in Denmark.

Last Friday I had my first meal with another family; at my friend Moris' house. I call him "Jeg," (I don't know if I already explained why I call him "Jeg"), so if I didn't, let me know. His family is really nice. They told me I was welcome anytime, so that's cool!

Remember the girl I told you about on the phone, the one from Germany, U.S., and Denmark? Well, it turns out she is not German, but Swiss. Oh yeah, and her name is Gudrun. Gad for short. She is not the most beautiful girl in the world, but she is really nice, and we get along very well. Last Friday we saw

LETTER 8 – CHECKING-OUT UNIVERSITIES

"The Adventures of Baron Munchhausen" together. It was a great movie. Well, it was kind of stupid, but we were kind of buzzed, so it turned out to be great. She's on the basketball team, and she is pretty good. She plays real aggressively, but when she is not playing, she is real shy.

Thanks for the animal postcards, especially the porcupine. When I told Anja I had eaten a rattlesnake (after I received the rattlesnake postcard), she nearly barfed! I liked the little saying you put on the porcupine card. You know it is kinda sad, I have only been gone two and a half month, and already, from the letters and phone calls (phone calls especially), I can tell that my friends and I are growing in different directions. From what I hear, its even happening between my friends. When I talked to Pia, she sounded like she could not give "a rat's ass" what happened to the guys. That kinda bummed me out. The only time things seemed to be the same is when I talked to Sam. Oh well, Sam and I have always had an interesting friendship. Well, that's it for now. I'll try to send a postcard from Costa Brava, so ADIOS until I get back. I miss you.

Love Peter

P.S. I was thinking the other day, not a day goes by that I don't think about you. Sheesh, it must be an obsession!

Oh yeah, in case you were wondering, I've developed some real good eating habits, and I'm starting to be able to make some decent meals. I can even make a steak the way you make it. Don't worry, I don't eat steak very often, though. I still could use a meal at our favorite restaurant at home. Love you.

Pet Shadow for me and give her a "Scooby" snack.

Adolescent Abroad

Moris was a Danish-American student like Peter. He had acquired the nickname "Jeg", roughly pronounced "yai", the Danish word for I. Moris had a very hard time pronouncing that word correctly in Danish, while the other Danish/American students caught on to the pronunciation quickly. Thus, Peter decided that Moris's nickname should be "Jeg."

By now some of Peter's friends had begun to refer to him as "Father Beast," because he was the "psychologist" among his class mates, the one other students would come to for advice.

I was not surprised to learn that Peter was the psychologist in his peer group. I had been studying clinical psychology while he was in high school, and we frequently discussed psychology. Consequently, Peter had acquired good psychological insight.

One reason Peter was interested in psychology was to try to understand Sam and himself. Peter and Sam had been best friends since third grade. They were both big and sensitive boys from single-parent homes. They tried to hide their vulnerability from other guys. For example, Peter worked out in the gym to get buff, and Sam was on the football team. Their efforts to convince the "real jocks" about their "macho" personalities failed, and they were often refer to as "nerds." They were both creative and spent much time drawing action figures and making up stories about them.

Letter 8 – Checking-out Universities

As a consequence of all the "psychology" talk we did in our family, Peter learned to articulate his thoughts and feelings well, and came across as a mature intelligent young man. Maybe that was why he and Gudrun became friends. In a phone call, he told me that she was a very mature and sensible young woman who had a calming affect on him. They became very close friends and kept in touch. When I met Gudrun, I realized that in many ways we were very similar, and Peter was comfortable with her because we were alike.

Gudrun would sometimes help Peter cook a good meal. Peter loved steaks, but in Denmark meat is very expensive, so steaks were a rarity for him. I only prepared steaks on special occasions at home and Peter was always thankful for those meals. It was fun to cook for Peter, he loved to eat and appreciated the effort I put into preparing a good meal.

Postcard from Costa Brava

Students have many more small vacations in Denmark than in the States. The Fall break, which Peter spent in Spain, was one of the additional breaks enjoyed by Danish students. Peter had looked forward to that trip, and I was happy he went. I wanted him to see as much of Europe as possible while living in Denmark.

October 18

Dear Mom.

I love it here. It's nice and warm, and the sun is perfect. I haven't even gotten sun burned. I just get more and more tanned. Gosh, the girls are beautiful! I'm here with Sean, Jess, and another guy named Michael. We are having a blast. But after four days, we are starting to get on each other's nerves. I went through Germany and France to get here. I must admit that France looked pretty nice. Miss you. I'll write more when I get back to Denmark.

Love Peter

The Fall break was initially implemented in the Danish schools when Denmark was an agrarian country and farmers needed their children to help harvest potatoes and rutabagas before the winters set in. In recent years, however, students frequently travel with their parents, or by themselves, to warmer climates in Southern Europe. Danes

love sun; the falls and winters are dark and cold, and spending time in warm, sunny places is a welcome break during the winter months.

Letter 9 – Birthday Party

Peter talked and wrote about his trip to Spain for a long time. Nila and I enjoyed hearing his stories. He was a good storyteller and described his adventures with great enthusiasm.

The next big event in Peter's life was his 18th birthday. Peter and I talked on the phone that morning. We were very sad to be apart on this special day. We had always made a big deal out of birthdays, and we reminisced about his past birthdays. His favorite was the thirteenth. That day I gave him permission to ditch school and took him around to all his favorite places in town. It was a great day until I locked my keys in the car. But we handled that little crisis well because we both were relaxed and having fun.

Peter celebrated his birthday with friends in Copenhagen. They took him out to eat and gave him presents. He was happy to have friends to party with and felt special being the center of attention.

October 23

Dear Mom.

Hello again, it's the night after I called. I just got back from having pizza with my friends from school. I got lots of presents: a box of chocolates, a box of brownies, a bag of rice-crispy treats, and best of all, a box of real CAPTAIN CRUNCH from Nella. She is a friend of mine who went to the U.S. for the fall holiday. Notice, everyone gave me food? I guess they know what I really need. Anja gave me 100 Danish Kroner, and I also got a letter from Dad with a check for $60. He wrote that he plans on sending me $100 every month while I'm here. He asked if that would be enough. I'm so happy he offered, so I'm taking it. It'll help a lot.

I hope you had a good time in Colorado, it sounds like you did. I wish I could have gone, it looks so pretty there.

Like I told you on the phone, I had a great time in Spain. I can't even begin to describe it to you. All day today, Sean, Jess, and I were telling everyone about our adventures in Spain. Everyone was cracking up. I'll try to get some pictures sent to you, so you can see what it was like. Also I finally bought a pirate flag and a coral necklace. The flag looks great in my room, and the necklace looks good on me when I am tanned, but I am already starting to lose the tan, so I guess I'll have to wait until spring to wear it again.

I almost forgot to tell you, I got my class picture taken. I am gonna order a packet and send some pictures to you and to Dad. I didn't like the picture, but my friends said it was good, so what the heck. Well, time for me to go to bed. I miss you and love you. Bye

Love Peter

P.S. Sorry my writing is so sloppy. I'm a bit out of practice and its midnight, so there!

Letter 9 – Birthday Party

Nila and I decided to take a small trip out of town while Peter was in Spain. We packed our bags and traveled to Colorado. I had always arranged several small trips for us during the year. It was something special to look forward to, and after each trip we cherished the memories and the fun we had. Peter enjoyed those trips, and even though he went to Spain, he still wished he could have traveled to Colorado with Nila and me.

Getting away, even for a few hours, was also fun for us. I frequently took Peter to the beach in California when he was little. We walked on the shoreline and pretended to look for stranded pirate ships. Since then Peter had been fascinated with pirates. During high school his room was decorated like a ship, but he never had a pirate flag until he found one in Spain.

Peter had many good memories from his childhood. He saw that time as safe and wondrous. After his father and I divorced he did not see his father much growing up, and he was pleased his father had remembered his birthday this time.

Letter 10 – Things Missed

I cherished all Peter's letters, but his next one was extra special. I read the paragraph designated as "Things I miss" many times. I was remembering our cozy times in front of the fireplace; singing to him in the mornings; and yelling when he ducked under the closing garage door. I felt very lucky having Peter in my life. He was a such a pleasurable "handful."

Halloween is Peter's favorite holiday. We always made a big deal out of that day. I would sew costumes for Peter and Nila and help them dress up.

October 31

Dear Mom.

Hi! I just called to tell you that I will be getting the financial aid now. Isn't that great. I'm glad they gave me the money already. I'm sure it takes a lot of stress off your back. Oh, speaking of money, here is some Francs for Nila...from France, of course. Just in case you are wondering, 3.10 Francs do not amount to diddly ___. I just thought she would like a piece of France, kinda see what it is like, ya know. She will like France, I think. Well, that makes nine countries I have visited. (U.S., Mexico, Japan, Denmark, Norway, Sweden, Germany, France, and Spain). Only 134 more, or so, to go. That's also three continents, only four more to go.

Adolescent Abroad

Time for THE THINGS I MISS -- You and Nila, my friends, my old bed, your Mexican food, cruisin' down Central Avenue, my high school, our fire place, the jaccuzzi, warmth, Price Club, slurpees, video games, "Dungeon Masters," you singing "♪♬ Good Morning, Good Morning tra la la lum dum ♬ Tra la la dum ♪♬" early on Saturday morning (about 11 o'clock), hearing you and Nila wake up to go jogging, arguing with you Mom about the faults of Socialism, having to push the button that closes the garage door and the running out of the garage before I get squished, good TV, country music, teasing Nila, trying to get Nila to play a game with us when my friends were over, RISK, when Joan brought over neat games that we didn't have, okay, Joan too, the river, and of course Ann! (Gosh, I wonder what you guys are thinking when you read this).

THE THINGS I DON'T MISS -- roaches, allergies, Tums, arguments with you Mom. Okay, I don't miss roaches, but I miss hunting them down and killin' 'em!

In case you forgot what I look like, I'll send a class picture when I get one. Meanwhile, try looking in the photo album or my year book.

Last Saturday, my school had a Halloween dance. By the way, we forgot to wish each other "Happy Halloween" on the phone, Mom!! Sean and I went as pirates. Guess who wore the eye patch? I also had the pirate flag with me that I got in Costa Brava. We looked pretty cool! We spend the night raping and pillaging! The girls didn't even resist too much. That threw us off guard, I started wondering what the hell kind of women they were. Then, I figured we just looked so savage they couldn't

Letter 10 – Things Missed

bring themselves to resist. I'll send a picture if I can get one. Well, gotta go to bed, I miss you and love ya!

Love Peter

P.S. I'm getting my first haircut in a foreign country sometime this week. I miss your haircuts too!

I was relieved to learn that Peter would be receiving financial aid from the Danish government. It was expensive to send Peter to a private school there. But I felt it was important that my children became familiar with Europe, and I encouraged them to live there for a while, in spite of the high cost.

Nila had expressed an interest in going to France to study after high school. She had already planned a trip there through the school for the following year. Peter felt she might appreciate a "taste" of France in advance, and sent her the left-over money from his trip through France to Spain.

Peter mentioned in his letter that he missed cruising on the main street in our town. It was a high school tradition to go cruising on Friday and Saturday nights. Peter did not have a car or a driver's licence, but he had many friends who invited him to cruise with them.

Another thing Peter missed was "Dungeon Masters" (Dungeons & Dragons). He loved that game, and often played it with his friends during high school. He was very embarrassed about playing it, however, because it was considered a nerdy game. Under no circumstances were Nila and I allowed to tell cute girls that he played Dungeons & Dragons.

Although Peter perceived himself as a nerd and was very shy around attractive girls, he was far from looking or acting like a typical nerd. He was very outgoing and handsome. He had beautiful blond curly hair, that I always had the pleasure of cutting. We both enjoyed those haircut times. Since I was his barber, I had some say-so about how his hair was styled, and it was always important for Peter that I liked the way he looked and dressed.

As soon as Peter moved to Denmark he began to miss my little cheerful morning song. Like most adolescents, Peter disliked waking up in the morning. Nevertheless, to teach him responsibility, I gave him an alarm clock to wake up by while he was in grade school. On weekends, however, Peter liked to sleep in, but I often woke him up by singing a little song for him. He pretended to hate that little tune.

Peter also missed Joan's new games. Joan was Nila's best friend. They met in Kindergarten and were inseparable for many years. She often came to our house to play with Nila. Peter and his friends used to think they were a nuisance. But when Joan brought a new game the girls were tolerated. Peter also missed Ann, the young woman he had a crush on prior to moving to Denmark.

Peter enjoyed discussing politics, and longed for one of our political debates. I frequently argued the merits of Socialism; Peter would point out the faults of that system. While in

Letter 10 – Things Missed

Denmark, he acquired an understanding of what Welfare Capitalism, the economic system of Denmark, was about. We continued our political discussions as soon as he came home.

When Peter's school held a Halloween party, he was initially confused when the girls appeared to welcome his "pirate attacks." He was unaccustomed to socializing with free-spirited women, and was inexperienced at the flirting game.

Thanks to the ancient magical elixer known as "Beer". Peter finds temporary – very temporary – love, and is changed forever.

Letter 11 – A Sexual Encounter

One important difference between Scandinavians and Americans is the way they feel about sex and violence. In Scandinavia, sex is talked about and displayed as openly in the media as violence is in the U.S. It is also very common for Scandinavian parents to discuss sex with their children in a frank and matter of fact way; and they feel more comfortable letting their children watch sex in a movie than they do violence.

As Peter and Nila grew up, I freely discussed sex and reproduction with them, and I never prohibited them from watching a movie that included a sex scene. However, I did not allow them to watch violence. Considering this cultural background, it was, therefore, not strange that Peter would shared his sexual experience with me in a free and comfortable manner. However, Peter's willingness to self-disclosure was also based on deep trust in me.

November 4

Dear Mom.

I'm so happy that I just had to write this letter. I was even tempted to call, but I had already called the U.S. twice this week. Besides I promised I'd send a picture of myself.

— BUT FIRST —
the boring stuff

Adolescent Abroad

Remember how I told you that I got my pictures from Costa Brava? Well, Sean and Jess were begging me to let them borrow the pictures since they wanted to show them to everyone, and I was done with school for the day. So I let them take the pictures, even though I really didn't want to. Well, they lost them of course, which pissed me off, but I have the negatives, the bad pictures, and the doubles. I'm making them pay for the pictures; I'm also gonna trust my feelings and not be persuaded so easily again.

I finally got hold of Juan, we had a great discussion. He said everything was shitty with the friends and stuff. I'm glad we talked. Besides Sam and Lisa, everyone freezes up on the phone, and it ends up being a big waste of money. Not with you, though. Juan said Pia got herself a boyfriend. I'm happy for her, she sounded pretty bummed in her first couple of letters to me, besides it takes me off the hook.

AND NOW FOR THE GOOD NEWS

It started Friday night. One of the guys in school had a friend visiting from Arkansas. Actually, she was here for a wedding. CAN YOU TELL WHERE THIS IS GOING? Anyway, this guy brought her along to the basketball game. We won again. All the guys are checking this new girl out, because she was gorgeous, plus she had this strong southern accent. BUT.....I wasn't paying too much attention to her, I was watching the game. After the game we saw "Pet Cemetery," and I still wasn't paying that much attention to her, because I was watching the movie. Finally, we all went home. I was on the bus with a bunch of my friends, and SHE was all they were talking about. So...

Letter 11 – A Sexual Encounter

The next day there was a party at one of my friends house, he's real cool. His dad is a general and works for the embassy, so he gets American food for me once in a while. After the party we, the whole school practically, were going to a pub to lend support for this rock band from our school. They were doing their first gig. But first we all had to get drunk, and I did. So I see this girl, Tina is her name, sitting by herself, and I decided to sit next to her and talk. I already liked her accent and the way she looked, and to top it off, she liked the same music I like. We were getting along great, and at the pub, even greater! We started singing country western songs, and my friends were trying to sing along, too, but they didn't know the words. By this time, every guy had given up on her, because they knew she was mine, so did I!

BY THE WAY, I DON'T WANT NILA TO READ THIS !

Then she says to me: "Let's go outside and get some fresh air." So off we went, and little did I know, we were being followed. Well, one thing let to another, and we started kissing and kissing, and then I noticed these heads pop out from around the corner. It was all my friends starring in amazement! So we took of to some secluded area and you can use your imagination from there on. But you may as well know, we didn't actually do it. But we did everything leading up to it, and I must say, I handled myself rather well. GOSH, I FEEL STRANGE TELLING you this... Anyway, I was so close, in fact, we were just searching for a place to ____. So if we had found one, then I would have, and therefore, I shall celebrate every Nov. 4th as LAYDAY. Too bad, she had to be home by twelve, otherwise...

So today, I'm kind of wandering around the house in utter amazement. I'm waiting for people to start calling me up and start making wise-cracks. And I am just dying to call someone at home and tell them about my conquest!! In case you were wondering... yes, I did love it, and it was as great, if not greater than I expected, and I plan on making a habit of it. I think I should stay drunk though, I'm pretty fearless that way. AAAAAHHHHH!

I'm filled with so much more confidence, and I feel like a barrier has just been lifted from "in front of me."

This is great!!!!!

Well, gotta go! I miss you lots and luv ya!!!

Love "the new" Peter

P.S. Hope you like the pictures from Costa Brava. Love you, Me

Peter was the leader of his peer group back home, and the one to keep the group together. He communicated well, was assertive, and helped his friends when they needed support. During his time in Denmark, his peer group at home was falling apart. This troubled Peter, and he tried to maintain the group cohesion while he was away.

Sam and Juan had been Peter's best friends since grade school. Peter had already called Sam, and finally got hold of Juan. Being the good group leader that he was, Peter wanted to talk to each individual to learn why the group was falling apart. His effort to reach his friends back home was also prompted by his wish to share his first sexual

Letter 11 – A Sexual Encounter

experience with them. I certainly understood its significance; Peter was very shy around young attractive women, and this sexual encounter though unconsummated marked a milestone in his life.

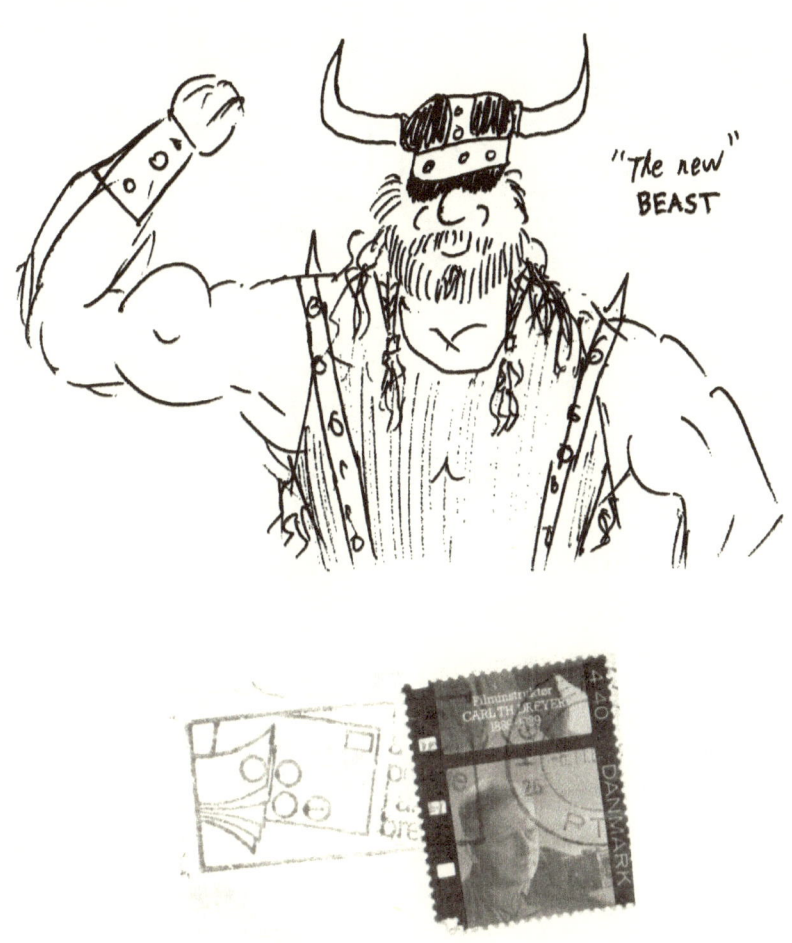

Letter 12 – Career Confusion

Peter was fiercely independent yet needed guidance concerning career choices. Because his school mates were applying to universities, Peter felt pressured to apply and make definite plans for his future, as well. Yet, he was ambivalent about attending university. I felt that Peter was not ready to choose a career and needed to come home rather than spend another four years away from Nila and myself. But Peter needed to make his own decision about his future plans.

November 19

Dear Mom.

Thank you so much for the letter with all the comics in it. Boy, a lot of them sure related to me. You should have seen me, I was cracking up. I'm sure Anja thought I had finally gone nuts. Then I called last Friday, too bad Nila wasn't there. I hate that. I also called Dad after I talked to you. That wasn't such a good conversation. Don't worry, Dad and I did not get into it with each other. The next day after I called I got a package from Florida Institute of Technology. I got to admit these prices scare me. You better believe I am gonna apply for financial aid and a student loan. God, the price of college seem like more money than I'll ever make in my life. Hell, sometimes I really wonder if an education is worth all that money. For the money I spend on college, I could have a pretty nice car and look educated. It's gonna cost $15,000 for the first year, and if I'm gonna get a

Bachelor's Degree, I'm looking at $60,000 for my education. Who knows how long it'll take me to pay that off. Then when I start up my own business, I'd have to take out another loan, probably for $100,000. Even if I don't start my own business, I'll be a middle-class person, who will struggle to keep myself and my family afloat, not to mention paying off my educational loans. Either way I look at it, it seems like I'm gonna pay through my ass, for the rest of my life.

Sorry if I seem bitter. It's just that I had trouble asking you for $10 when I wanted to have some extra fun on the weekend. Then I came out here, and that probably puts a pretty big dent in your wallet. Finally, I got that financial aid so you don't have to pay another $3,000 just so I can live. I don't know, should I kiss a college education goodbye or what?

What it boils down to, is that I don't like putting this kind of burden on you. I'm actually an adult now (I know that's gotta be hard for you to accept, but 18 is the legal age), and I'm still living off you. It doesn't seem right.

The more I look at these prices, the more attractive the military looks. I mean, shit, all I have to do is give up four years of my life and learn what I want to learn. Four years of taking orders doesn't seem too bad compared to $60,000. It's like getting paid $15,000 a year to do what I'm told, plus I get a paycheck from Uncle Sam on top of that. There is also the GI bill that would pay for part or all my college education after I'm done with the military. That's assuming I want to go to college after the military, of course.

LETTER 12 – CAREER CONFUSION

I know you really have your heart set on me going to college, and I'm sorry if this letter kind of upsets you. But reality just kind of walked up and slapped me in my face. I hope you don't think I'd be any less of a person because I didn't go to college, like dad. I believe I'm already beyond that point, and that it isn't the level of education that makes a person, although some people might think so. But I don't need those kind of people that would judge me because of something like that. Let me know what you think soon, OK, because time is running out. I have to have a definite plan for my future soon.

On to better things. Well, by now all my friends know Nila is a model and they are as anxious as I am to see her pictures. Boy, I'm so proud of her. In a way I envy her. She is taking control of her future now, instead of letting the future control her (like it is with me). Yep, pretty smart sister I raised. I know why she is so smart, too. It's because when she was little, I always tried to sucker her out of her money. It's true.

Well, I am freezing my ass off, and it is probably starting to get cold at home too. So when you light up the fireplace, be sure to play with the fire, or put your hands through the flames for me. OK!

Love Peter

Peter loved to acquire new knowledge, but worried about paying for a university education, and felt ashamed to ask me for money. He had always been torn between being a carefree young boy and the caretaker of Nila and me. The prospect of spending four years at a university, without

financial independence, was almost unbearable for him. The conflict between his wish to learn and need to be independent, made it difficult for him to visualize a future for himself.

I worried about Peter's inability to see the correlation between getting a good university degree and a good profession. When he was younger, Peter had many dreams and creative ideas about what to do when he grew up. After he moved to Denmark, he could no longer see a direction for himself. His confusion partly stemmed from living in a foreign country, and being surrounded by students of a higher socio-economic class and stronger academic backgrounds than his own.

I tried to be very supportive of Peter during this difficult time. I knew it would pass, and that his next letter would contain new problems about growing up. He was no longer the little boy in charge of building fires on cold winter evenings, who amused himself kindling the fire and melting marshmallows, performing his "fireman" duties.

Letter 13 – Thanksgiving

Winters are long and dark in Denmark. Daylight meekly interrupts the long night around nine in the morning and retreating in embarrassment mid-afternoon. Thick clouds often hide the sun for a month at a time. Many Danes find these dark winter months depressing, but they welcome the first snowfall and always wish for a white Christmas. Snow does not stay on the ground very long, however, because temperatures are, typically, just above freezing.

It was the first day of snow when Peter wrote this letter, and it was also Thanksgiving day. Although Thanksgiving is not a Danish holiday, Peter took the day off from school and was able to enjoy the falling snow. It never snowed where we lived in the U.S., but Peter had many fun memories from ski trips we had taken. Now he could experience how it was to live in a climate where winters were cold and snowy.

November 23

Dear Mom.

Wow! What a day this has been. It is Thanksgiving day, so the day was already off to a good start. I'll start at the beginning. First of all, the Americans at my school all planned to take the day off since it is an American holiday. The Israelis take the Jewish holidays off, so why shouldn't we. None of us had really planned to do anything on that day besides sleep in. The days are getting real short, so it is hard to wake up in the mornings. So there I was sleeping when suddenly I was awaken by a disturbing dream. It wasn't a nightmare, just a disturbing dream. I couldn't sleep after that, so I ended up waking up at the same time I usually do. That sucked.

Next, I decided I was hungry, so I headed upstairs. The mailman had already been by, and guess who I got a letter from?...Mrs. Thomas, my old Japanese teacher. I was so happy. Then, I went into the dinning room to eat and started reading my letter. She was talking about how she knew how I felt about moving, since she just moved to Singapore. But I was thinking to myself: "Hey, I'm completely adjusted to this place, I've got the whole routine down, I'm even liking it!" Just then I felt something falling outside... SNOW!!

Well, so much for my routine, I thought. Then, I went outside to let the snow fall on my face. It was so beautiful. That was the first snow of the year, and it was nothing but slush by the end of the day. Tomorrow, however, we are suppose to get a big snowstorm.

After all that I went into town alone, because nobody wanted to do anything, or I couldn't get hold of them. I messed around for a while, spent some money and then said to myself: "What a waste, I may as well have gone to school." So I went home. All the while I was bothered by the way my trench coat was fitting, and wishing that the jacket you were gonna send me would come. To my surprise, there it was, waiting for me at home. It fits great. I like it. Thank you!!

Anja was all excited about the popcorn popper, but the transformer only works up to 1000 watts, and the popper is 1440 or 1460 watts, so it doesn't work and a transformer out

Letter 13 – Thanksgiving

here is so expensive that she could buy four popcorn poppers for the price of a transformer. I felt so bad, but she really was thankful for it and she liked the wreath you made for us. I love all of my presents. Thank you. Hey, what good timing you have. I was just running out of shampoo and conditioner.

Well, to top it all off, toward the end of the day (now) I started feeling a little homesick. So....since it is Thanksgiving I think I'll call. [*He called me*]

AAHHH! I feel so much better now, but I hate saying goodbye. Too bad you can't come out here for Christmas, but at least Nila can. I sure miss her. Boy, it made me mad when I heard the agent rejected her. What an asshole! When I get back, I'm gonna get the guys together and we're gonna bust the place down to the ground, OK.!

Well, I have told you almost everything, so I guess I better go. Thanks again for all the presents! I love you and miss ya!

Love Peter

The big box of Christmas presents I had sent to Peter and Anja in September finally arrived. I included a warm winter jacket for Peter to replace the leather jacket he brought from the States, which had been stolen at his school. It had been his favorite jacket. He had wanted a black leather jacket for many years, but they were too expensive for our budget. However, when Peter turned seventeen I wanted to celebrate in style, anticipating his departure to Denmark. I bought the jacket and casually placed it on his bed. When he came home from school that day and walked into his room I heard

a loud scream. He rushed into the kitchen to hug me. It was a special moment. When the jacket was stolen, Peter called home crying. In Copenhagen clothes are much more expensive than in the States, so I promised to send another warm jacket as soon as possible. Peter and I frequently went shopping together, and I knew the style of clothing he liked.

The hot air popcorn popper was for Anja, and because electricity is different in Denmark than in the States, I included a transformer in the Christmas box. Nila finally brought the correct transformer when she came to visit Peter for Christmas. Both Peter and Anja used the popcorn popper frequently. Peter later told me that toward the end of each month, when he was running out of money, he ate popcorn for dinner.

Nila also ate popcorn for dinner when we wanted to loose a few pounds. But she had not lost enough weight to satisfy a modeling agency in town. When Peter learned that she had been rejected, he was angry. He always felt Nila's pain and wanted to protect her. Peter knew revenge was unsound, but when angry, his initial reaction was retaliation. Fortunately, he always talked to me before he acted, and our conversation always calmed him down.

Peter's Japanese teacher from high school moved to Singapore shortly after Peter's trip to Japan. She had been instrumental in arranging his visit and worked closely with him while he was president of the Asian club. Peter felt very close to her and they kept in contact for many years.

Section III. Holiday Blues

This section consists of three letters written between the end of November and the middle of February. Peter was very homesick and depressed during this time. Letters were scarce, but we talked more frequently on the phone, and our conversations helped us deal with the holiday blues.

If Peter's attitude had been more positive, his holidays might, actually, have been exciting. First, Nila came to visit, and then his childhood friend, Lana, flew in. He also enjoying a few vacation days in Sweden with my brother and his family. Nevertheless, for Peter there was no place like home for the holidays, and he made no bones about that in the coming letters.

gasp!
uunngg!
cough!
cough!
sneeze!

BARF BUCKET

← used Kleenex

Letter 14 – The Flu

I always encouraged both Peter and Nila to talk to me, or to each other about their concerns. As soon as they came home from school I would ask them about their day, how their friends were doing, what they had learned, and so on. I strongly believed that problems easily could be resolved by "talking them out." Consequently, Peter had been conditioned to talk to me about everything. Physical separation from me did not deter that habit. What changed was the way we communicated, and we both looked forward to receiving letters from each other.

Although Peter was outgoing, he was also a reserved individual, sharing his thoughts and feelings with only a select few. Thus, while Peter wrote me about feeling depressed and inferior, his friends perceived him as being cheerful and confident. Nila and I were the only ones aware of the misery Peter experienced during the next couple of months.

November 27

Dear Mom.

Sorry, this is another one of these bad letters. To start it off, I'm sick, real sick, damn sick, and I hate it. I was just sick at the beginning of this month, and here I go again. It was because of a snowball fight I had with some other guys. I played so hard, I started sweating (and you know how I sweat), so now I'm sick. I hate staying here all day, it's so boring, no one to talk to or to get me a glass of juice, or make me a bowl of soup. I also missed a math test, a social anthropology test, and a physics test. They rarely give make-up tests here (only if a lot of people miss the test). So now I'm starting to feel like a failure again.

Well, you know how I am when I get depressed. I start depressing myself even more. All I do is think about the bad things. Believe me, that list is long!! I don't even know where to start....Oh yeah, I did start.....I'm sick!

2. The weather is really shitty, all the snow has turned into slush, and now it is hailing, and the sky is black. It's just one of those days.

3. I don't know what to get you for Christmas.

4. I'm really homesick.

5. Sam's visit. I was talking to some people who had gone "interrailing," and they said it's cheaper than going on other tours. All you need is an interrail pass and $1,000 for food, youth hostels, entertainment, souvenirs, etc. I just freaked! Where the hell is Sam suppose to get that kind of money. I might be able to do it, if I really save up. God, that is one thing I hate about my friends out here, they are all so rich...money is nothing to them. All they have to do is ask, and they shall receive. It really sucks, because every time I start getting to know someone, and become close, our social classes collide. I have to explain to these people what it is like not to live in a mansion. Mom, you should have seen it when I tried to tell my friends that I was thinking of going into the military because college was too expensive. All of a sudden they started to treat me like I was a lesser form of life. They started asking me

Letter 14 – The Flu

questions, such as what my parents do, how much money they make, do I get along with my parents, all kinds of stupid questions that really aren't their business. It's like they are starting to analyze me. That made me really think that I can never be best friends with these people. The girls are a little better than the guys. They seem a little more sincere about their concerns about me. But I can still just imagine how they talk about me. "Peter, yeah he sure is a nice guy, lots of fun to be around, but..." So anyway, I feel like I'm being brought back to how I was when I came here. Does that make sense? It's like the person that I became while I have been here, isn't the same anymore, because people don't think of me the same way they used to.

Anja and I get along, but she rags on me every once in a while about the dumbest things. One time she said I was "cheating," because after I took a shower, I didn't wipe off the hot water faucet as well as the cold one. (I have to wipe the whole bathroom every time I take a shower). I had to explain to her what "cheating" meant, but she still goes by her own definitions, so whenever I do something wrong, I'm "cheating." I am getting very tired of being called a cheater! What sucks, I can't yell back at her because I'm renting her room, so I'm stuck. Many times I've just retreated into my room and asked myself; "What in the HELL are you doing here!"

Boy, all that was just # 5 on my list of depressing thoughts. I'm starting to wish I hadn't made all those other plans for Christmas (Lana, Nila, Sweden, etc) and instead just flown back for about a week. I think it would do me a lot of good. The only problem would be saying goodbye again. Well, if it turns out that Sam won't be able to afford the trip to Europe, I'm heading straight home, forget touring and all that. I've had it with this place. I don't belong here, I belong in the States. This is why I'm not into the idea of being a diplomat anymore. I just want things to be stable. I want to be confidant in whatever I'm doing, and not feel like a fool every time someone starts speaking Danish, and I have to tell them I can't speak their language. Then, they start speaking English because they can hear my accent. I'm just so sick of all this!

I don't know, maybe it's just these winter months that bum me out. If so, I can't wait for spring. Don't get all alarmed when you read this letter Mom, like you did with the last sad letter. I'm sure things will be better by the time you get the letter. OK! I'm bound to feel totally depressed every once in a while. It also helps to tell someone, or in this case, write someone. I miss you so, so much. I love you.

Love Peter

Peter was rarely sick as a child. His treatment when ill was to stay in bed and sleep or read. He was not allowed to watch television or talk extensively with his friends on the phone. I prepared his favorite chicken soup and brought him plenty of juice. That type of treatment cured him quickly, and he could not wait to see his friends and be part of the action at school again. In Denmark, Peter felt even more lonely and isolated when he was sick, and, like many adolescents, he was egocentric, hyper-sensitive, and sometimes unreasonable in his judgment of others. However, once he began

Letter 14 – The Flu

talking about things that bothered him, he understood that he was overreacting.

In his self pity Peter felt that his shower chores were unreasonable. However, the water in Denmark is very hard, and it was important that Peter dry the faucets and walls after each shower to avoid formation of large calcium deposits. Peter was not used to cleaning in this extensive manner, and frequently failed to do a good job.

Lana and Nila were coming to visit Peter for Christmas, and they all planned to go together to visit my brother in Sweden, where he managed a restaurant at a ski resort. Peter and Nila were used to helping my brother during our summer trips to Scandinavia. He paid for their airfare, and in turn they helped in his restaurant. This was also the plan for the upcoming holiday. Initially, that plan sounded good to Peter, but as the holidays neared he got very homesick and wanted to spend Christmas at home.

Letter 15 – Nila Arrives

I believed that to fully learn about a foreign country, one should stay there for at least one full year, in order to participate in the holidays unique to that place. Consequently, I felt Peter should spend Christmas in Denmark; there were no plans that he come home. Besides, traveling during the holidays was too expensive for us.

I worked hard to give Peter and Nila a comfortable home and a cultured upbringing. Little by little our living conditions had improved and Peter was very appreciative of our progress. I always emphasized that we were a team, and without their help I would be unable to make it. During the holidays Peter reminisced about our difficult times and wished he could be home to share the good life we now enjoyed.

December 18

Dear Mom.

Hi! Sorry I haven't written for a while, but I thought you were probably getting tired of the sad letters, so I decided to wait until my mood improved. Unfortunately, my mood isn't improving, so I'll write anyway.

But first! How was your big party? I hope it was lots of fun. Wow, that is the first big party you have had for a long time. Weren't you nervous? I'm happy for you, I think having a party is a good (very good) sign that things are improving. Boy, we sure have come a long way. I figured our situation would never improve after you and dad divorced, and now look at us. I'm growing up, you have a good car, a nice house, a dog, a fire place, and good friends. I wish I was there to eat the leftovers from the party.

Well, Nila is in Sweden now. It was so good to see her. She and I have never been apart for this long. I must have said a hundred times: "God, I can't believe you're actually here! It was like no matter how hard I tried to believe it, I couldn't. It seemed like such a long time ago that we were together, that I couldn't believe I actually have a family. Boy, this loneliness has really gotten to me. Still, I was so happy. Then, as soon as she came, I had to let her go again. That was a terrible feeling, because I could tell she really didn't want to leave. After she left I started crying. I was feeling both her sadness and my own sadness. At least, I will be with her again in a week. Well, it was so nice of your brother to give her the ticket to come over here.

Anyway, I have already taken my math and history exams, and tomorrow I take my social anthropology exam and my physics exam, then Wednesday I take my Danish exam. The math exam was last Thursday, the day Nila arrived. I had studied hard and felt that my understanding of math was at a new high for this year. I felt very confident during the test and finished it with little difficulty, with the exception of a few problems. So today Gudrun called me and told me my grade. I'm too freaking ashamed to tell you, but rest assured, it was shitty!!! She told me not to worry, because the teacher grades by a curve. I'm feeling really bad though, because I had never felt that I would do any good on a math test until this one, then look what

Letter 15 – Nila Arrives

happened. Shit, I don't know what to do now, I really like the teacher and the students, and I can't just drop out. Remember all that newly gained confidence I had after my little adventure on November 4th? *[See letter #11]*. Well, that's long gone. I'll tell you, this year is not turning out to be what I thought it would be. I can see someone asking me what I did after high school... "Oh, I just took off to a foreign country to live alone and gradually destroy myself." I will not leave until the year is finished, though, because if I did, that would be my ultimate loss. So, now I will begin to view this year as an experiment to see how much torture I can take.

I'm not even done yet. I got a letter from the bank today showing how much I've been spending. Yes, you guessed it, I screwed that up, too. That doesn't bother me so much, though, because I have figured out how to improve that situation earlier today and still have money for the trip through Europe with Sam, if he comes; if he doesn't, I'm out of here. Boy, having to leave Nila, not being with you over the holidays, my progress in school (or rather lack thereof), and my foolish money management all in a few days!!!! This place causes me too much pain, and I'll take it no matter how bad it gets, but I'll tell you one thing, I'm not coming back to this place for a long looooonnnggg time!

Anyway, before you start to puke at another one of my depressing letters, I want to thank you for all the back-up presents you send with Nila. I miss you so much. I would give anything to be able to go back just for Christmas. I feel terrible that you have to work for the holidays. Oh yes, and thanks for the college stuff. Embry-Riddle in Arizona looks great. It even has army and air force ROTC, if I decide to learn how to fly helicopters or jets. Darn, another decision to make.

Well, I leave for Sweden this Thursday and head back the 26th to pick up Lana. Then, we'll go up there again the 30th, and all of us (Nila, Lana, and I) will come back here again January 3rd. This will be a busy vacation. I cannot wait for spring. I have the feeling things will get better then, they better get better. I gotta' go, I love you so much. Say "Hi" to everyone for me. Bye.

Love Peter

Peter was lonely and depressed but hoped that spring would improve his attitude. During the dark winter months Scandinavians long for Spring, which renews their energy and zest for life.

I also felt lonely during Christmas, and offered to work every day during that Christmas season. Preoccupying myself with work left little time to think about Peter and Nila. I also decided to have a big Christmas party to occupy my time. Peter recalled how I used to be nervous before our parties. He and Nila always helped me and now he wondered how I had managed without them.

"I love Yule Brew!" — Yule Viking!

Christmas Card

For most Scandinavians, Christmas eve is the most sacred event of the season. A dinner for close family members is the tradition. People eat duck, pork roast, or turkey, and a delicious rice pudding for dessert. After dinner, everyone joins hands and all walk in a circle around the Christmas tree. They sing religious Christmas hymns and popular Christmas songs. Finally, presents are opened, one by one, and everyone sits around talking and telling old Christmas stories. I had maintained the Danish Christmas traditions, and Peter missed that special time with his family.

Christmas

Dear Mom,

Well, I'm writing all my Christmas cards now, believe me I've got a lot to write (45). Finally, I've come to your card. This is the most important card of all. I can't express how much I'm gonna miss spending the holidays with you. But I still hope you have a...

Merry Christmas

+

Happy New Year!!

And keep playing all those Christmas tunes, I miss them, too. Well, I guess after this it's just gonna get easier and easier, and before I know it, I'll be home! (I hope).

I love you so much. Have fun and drink lots of Gluk (hope that is spelled right).

Love Peter

Peter loved keeping in touch with family and friends. This was even more important to him at Christmas than at any other time of the year. To write 45 Christmas cards was quite an undertaking for him. He filled every blank space on each card. Oh well, I am the same way.

Peter mentioned that I should drink lots of "Gluk." The correct English spelling is Glogg. It is a traditional Scandinavian spiced wine, prepared at Christmas to keep people warm and happy. I make Glogg every Christmas; it is part of our Danish Christmas tradition.

Letter 16 – A Clean Shave

Peter and I talked several times during the holidays. Christmas had been difficult; we missed each other very much. However a new year had started, and Peter looked forward to new beginnings. I was happy to have Nila back home. She had enjoyed her stay with Peter, and reassured me that he was doing well.

───◇───

January 7

Dear Mom,

Sorry it's been so long since you've gotten a letter from me, but as you probably already know, I was pretty busy this vacation. Anyway, Lana is packing now and this is the first letter I've written this year.

Wow, there is so much to tell, I don't know where to start! Ok! Ok! Ok! I'll start with "I shaved my beard off!" AAAARRRGGG! It's easier not having a beard, and I think more girls are looking at me, but I just don't feel comfortable without it. I don't know why, but I'm gonna grow it back during the winter break. Oh yeah, I'm also in a much better mood than I have been the last, who knows how many, letters, I don't know why. I MISS YOU!

I already told you how lousy our Christmas was and I'm sure Nila already told you about New Years eve. That little shit, she just broke my heart. I have nothing against her growing up, I just don't want her doing it while I'm around! It was so nice seeing her again, and I cried when Lana and I dropped her off at the airport (I hate goodbyes). I wish so bad I could see you again, but then I'd have to drop you off at the airport. AAARRRGG! I can't wait to come home.

Did Nila tell you how Lana and I climbed the mountains in total darkness and with the poor weather conditions. Man, that was a bitch, but I kept telling myself that if I can get to the top of the mountains, then I'll be able to overcome all my challenges and succeed in life, well, at least for the next decade. In ten years, I'll have to climb a bigger mountain or do something weird like that.

After Lana leaves, I'm gonna start getting my shit together (eat more corn!). I got a lot of problems coming up with money and college and whether or not to go into the service. Since you told me that all the pilots you talked to are bored with flying, I'm starting to wonder whether flying is for me, or if I would be able to hack it. God, I still have so many inferiority complexes, (sounds like small apartment buildings). I think I have more since I've moved here, because I'm afraid to fail and worry about impressing my new friends and stuff like that. But I am gonna work real hard on getting rid of them.

I just started realized that last night, or actually this morning. Lana and I were up until 7:00 in the morning, talking about everything. We even talked about why Lana moved away, and how the guys and I blew her off that summer. That was a tough conversation. We also talked about all the stuff she's doing as far as getting her career in the theater going, and how I'm getting nowhere. Boy, that made me feel like a worthless pile of shit. But as I've said before, the closer I get to Spring, the better

Letter 16 – A Clean Shave

things will be, and I've got a real nice summer planned, so at least, I have something to look forward to.

I have been thinking about you all vacation, and I decided to send a few "funnies," since you always send some to me. Ok yes, and a few clippings out of the paper, they are some of the things the movie critics are saying about the "Accidental Tourist." Who says I don't think of you.

My second report card should be coming around soon. I don't think it will be too good, but that is something else I gotta work on...

Make sure to give me the latest news on the Pan Am flight in your next letter OK [*the Lockerbie disaster*]. Wow, last year "exciting," wasn't it? I figure, with all the new global development, we are either gonna have world peace, or the world is gonna be trapped in some serious problems. Who knows!

By the way, when you get my report card (I haven't received a copy yet, and it might be a while), keep in mind that I have learned so much this year in academia and in everyday living, that I could still blow the socks off almost all Americans my age, when it comes to those subjects. It's just these European International Baccalaureate students that make me look bad. God, they are so smart. OK, and I love you. (Remember I always used to tell you that, when I was a little kid and thought I'd be in trouble). Did I tell you that Lana and I saw the "Northern Lights" on New Years Eve when we climbed the mountains. They were awesome.

Adolescent Abroad

Well, tomorrow Lana leaves. We've had some good times, but I wish Nila could have stayed that long as well. Lana has been sick most of the time here, and she can be a little annoying sometimes. But she is my friend, and I guess I gotta take the bad with the good, eh! Anyway, it'll be nice to have things back to normal. I better sign off now. I love you and miss you so much. Hope to hear from you soon. Say "Hi" to everyone OK. Bye

Love Peter

I feared flying, and putting my kids on an airplane caused me a great deal of anxiety. My apprehension increased shortly before Nila and Lana's flight to Scandinavia, when Pan Am Flight 103 exploded over Lockerbie, Scotland. A bomb had been planted on the plane. We were shocked by the incident, and frightened that further attacks would happen.

Nila and Lana arrived safely in Denmark and Peter had enjoyed their visits. Nila was growing up, however, and she flirted with one of the ski lift workers at my brother's hotel. At the New Year's Eve party they kissed. This upset Peter; he was not ready for his little sister to grow up.

On New Year's Eve, Lana and Peter climbed a nearby mountain, in freezing weather and total darkness. When they reached the top, they saw the Northern Lights dancing about the sky. It was a spectacular sight that Peter talked enthusiastically for many years. It almost made up for the trauma his first Christmas away from home had caused him.

Letter 16 – A Clean Shave

Over the years Lana and Peter had spent many memorable times together. Peter and his friends played at Lana's house during grammar school and into high school. She was one of their buddies, an only child, who had all the toys Peter and his friends wanted but did not have. In high school, the boys became envious of Lana for having all these toys. The summer between their Freshman and Sophomore years, they stopped playing with her, and Lana was devastated. When school started again the guys continued to ignore her. Lana was deeply hurt. She chose to move and live with an aunt in another state. Peter realized the pain she felt and quickly rekindled their relationship through letters and phone calls. They kept in close contact for many years.

I appreciate the fine friendships Peter has developed. He is a great friend; fun loving, caring, and genuine. I often reminisce about the times he and I chummed around. When going to movies, we took turns choosing what to see. One movie I chose was "The Accidental Tourist." That movie became an inside joke between us. Peter hated it, and frequently reminded me how he had "suffered" through that movie.

Section IV. Girls

Peter suddenly discovered that cute girls were almost like boys, and reports on his new observation in the following eight letters, written between the middle of January and the end of March. He began to party on weekends, and to someone unfamiliar with the Danish culture, it may seem as if Peter and his friends drank excessively. However, Danes prize their beer and are socialized to like the taste at an early age.

Beer drinking is a rite of passage into adulthood. It also helps adolescents overcome the awkwardness they initially feel around the opposite sex. Peter hoped that a beer buzz could ease his shyness around girls, and he eagerly make up for his previous "party deprivation."

Letter 17 – Wham, Girls!

Several girls wanted to go steady with Peter during high school, but the ones he liked, the beautiful popular girls, he shied away from. Occasionally, Peter would send the girl of his heart a beautiful poem and tell her how much he adored her personality and beauty. The girls never responded positively to Peter's innocent cavaliering. Nevertheless, when he was in love, Peter floated on air, especially if his beloved gave him an occasional smile.

January 15

Dear Mom.

Hello, I miss you!! I almost called you, but I don't want you to get bored of hearing from me. You probably wonder why I don't write so often. Well, the truth is that I'm way behind on my writing and I've been real busy with everything else out here. That is good, because the busier I am, the quicker time flies, and the sooner I'll be home.

Oh, but get this! I'm on an upswing and I'm starting to like it here again. This recent turn of events is due to several new additions to our group of friends. GIRLS!!! These chicks are great, they are just like Jess, Sean, and myself; fun-lovin', wild, horny, but they are girls!!!. We just got invited to one of their parties, and WHOOOM, we began to see them in a new light. It's weird, they have always been going to our school, but our groups never really paid attention to each other. Anyway, we partied a while, at one of the girls' house and got to know each other's names and stuff. Then, we went to a pub, and that's when the action started. Of course we were all pretty buzzed. There were about fifteen of us, and once we had been there for a while, a girl named Anna from Norway, suggested a game. We all had to sit around a table (boy-girl-boy-girl). She took a matchstick, tore off the explosive part, stuck it in her teeth, and passed it to the guy next to her, in his teeth. I was like WHOA! A girl named Laila was sitting next to me. I was thinking to myself, UH-OH, this girl's not bad, what the hell is she doing sitting next to me? Anyway, back to the game. Every time the matchstick made its way around without dropping, it was broken in half, and so on and so on. You can see where this would lead. So Laila and I kept playing while most of the others quit. And it didn't stop there. Finally, we all went back to one girl's house to spend the night. Laila and I cuddled up, it was pretty nice (that was really an understatement). We just talked and cuddled, and kissed. What's cool, we are not even boyfriend and girlfriend, neither do we want to be. God, I LOVE A LOT OF THINGS ABOUT THIS COUNTRY. And this was only Friday.

We left the next morning, and I went home to take a shower and then went to the airport to see Jeg off. That was his last day in Denmark, bummer. Got home about 12:00 and slept till 9:00 PM. I was late for a poker game, so I headed there as soon as I woke up. We hardly ever play poker, it's just a party night for the guys where we all get drunk, dance around to all kinds of music (none of us can dance to save our lives), and basically have a good time, without having to worry about scoring with some chick. I think it is called male bonding, because we all talk a lot and really get to know each other. Well, I didn't get

Letter 17 – Wham, Girls!

out of there until Sunday morning. I got home and slept all day and have been awake since. It is now Monday evening, and I'm getting pretty tired.

I will tell you, these parties keep getting better and better. If we are playing "Matchsticks" today, imagine what we'll be playing by the end of the year! Oh well, I'm up for it.

Whatever you do, don't get all worried and concerned, OK. I really need these parties to keep me going. Some concerned parent called the principal, and that really screwed things up for that kid. So if you are concerned, take it up with me, OK. I love you.

Oh, and don't worry about the girls, they seem OK. You know what is weird, I was thinking about how I was, before I came here, and how I never would have done stuff, like what I am telling you about now. I wanted a nice "relationship" with a princess of a woman. Well, those days are over, for a while anyway. Gosh, it's weird to think back on all that stuff, it seems like with every letter I get (from my old friends), there is more and more talk about who is backstabbing who. I don't want that. I wish they could experience the fun I'm having. I think one reason it's so fun is that we are not hurting each other. We are just a bunch of fun-lovin', wild, horny, teenagers. Other times I feel kind of irresponsible, like I should be the same as I was when I got here. Then, I think, "Hey, I'll bet mom used to do the same stuff." Well, you turned out OK. All in all, I'm glad we decided to send me out here. Through all the pain and the wildness, I think I'm a better person now. WOW, I sure think differently when I'm in a good mood, eh!

Adolescent Abroad

I better go to bed. I love you and miss you so much. That is one thing I will always return to, you. Write back soon, OK. Or call once in a while. I love you, bye!

Love Peter

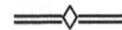

I was delighted to learn that Peter's mood had improved. I used to have lots of fun in Copenhagen when I was his age. I am very thankful for those happy memories, and attribute part of my maturity and sense of responsibility as an adult, to my happy and playful youth. I encouraged Peter to have fun and take advantage of the liberal and fun-loving life Copenhagen had to offer.

The young women at Peter's school were more liberal and sexually open-minded than those Peter socialized with during high school, and he was both excited and apprehensive about them. Nevertheless, Copenhagen was a wonderful and safe place for Peter to unfold.

"I love you!"

Letter 18 – Grades

Peter was blossoming. In the fall, he had been concerned with choosing a career. It had also been a difficult time because he was an outsider among his peers. During the dark winter months, however, Peter overcame his despair, and emerged with a new zest for life. He even began to understand that on a psychological and emotional level, he was stronger and more mature than many of his friends. This realization gave him the confidence to make decisions about his future.

January 21

Dear Mom.

Hello again! I miss you. I just got the package with the college stuff, and two days ago, I got a letter from Nila. HURRAY, you got a CD player, that is great, I can't wait to play with it (and "hog" it).

Thanks for the college stuff Mom, but I am seriously thinking about going to Junior College. I think that would be a good idea. It's better than wasting time and money studying something I don't want to do. I did look through the package, though. I hope you are not upset about the Junior College decision, after all the running around you did, getting applications and the like. We can save them for when I do apply.

Well, I finally got my report card (2 Bs, and 3 Cs). I know that's not good, but it is a lot better than I expected, believe me. I guess I'm doing better than I thought. Whew, I have no self-esteem (psycho-term), so I keep puttin' myself down. I think it is because I am surrounded by so many talented people. They're all so smart, most play musical instruments (very well), and speak at least three languages fluently. Shit, how can I compete with that. I guess I gotta' learn how to play the drums or guitar, learn Danish perfectly, pick up another language, such as French or German, or take up Japanese again. Whew, that's a lot of work. It doesn't seem that bad though, when I just write it down, and it fits on a couple of lines. Anyway, I'll try to improve my grades.

Well, onto better things, like GIRLS!! Remember last week the girl, Laila, I mentioned? Well, things are getting better. Actually, we did not talk at all during the school week, but everyone was teasing us about last weekend. And unbeknown to us, someone had taken a picture of us and started to pass it around in school. It was kinda funny, but we just totally shied away from each other, just an occasional "Hi" in the halls. Friday, we had lunch together, and that night we all went to a pub in Svanemollen. Unfortunately, Gudrun came too. She likes me, but I don't like her "that" way. Well, by some strange coincidence Laila and I sat next to each other. We were getting real friendly, but Gudrun kept interrupting. She finally left though, she was pissed. I kinda felt bad, but she knows I only like her as a friend. What do you think, should I feel like an asshole or not? Well, we were both pretty tipsy, and while I was busy explaining to her why Reagan should have been TIME magazine's man of the decade, instead of Gorbachev, the next thing I knew, we're kissing. God, to this day I don't know how it happens, it just does. After a while we all left the pub and went to the train station. Laila's

Letter 18 – Grades

train was going in the opposite direction of mine. She told me to come home with her, her parents were not home. I wondered why she wanted me to do that. BUT... I didn't, (maybe next weekend) because my friend Jess had just been rejected by the girl he has been after for a few weeks. She wanted to date Sean instead, and the two of them were nowhere to be found, so Jess was kind of pissed, and I figured I should look out for him. Of course I regret that now, because Laila is going to be in Holland until the 25th with everyone else in Model United Nations, so I won't see her for a while. I used to be in Model United Nations too, but I quit, because there were too many rules. Pretty stupid, eh!

I guess I better tell you about Laila. First her dad is the Head of Communication for one of the foreign embassies here. He is in on all the spy stuff with bugs and junk like that. Laila is small, about 5' 4" – 5' 5", blonde, not a goddess, but really fun, so that makes up for it. She has lived in Quebec, Morocco, and Denmark, and she has traveled all over Europe. She speaks English, Canadian-French, and Arabic (I think). She insists she speaks Canadian-French because that is to French what American is to English, and she doesn't like the French. "They are too stuck up on themselves," she says. She thinks her "French" sounds better than the French spoken in France; more strong words. Even my history teacher dislikes the French. He thinks French nationalism gets in the way of progress that could be made in the European Common Market. Since France is such a big country, it has a lot of representatives (power) in the European Parliament, council and commission, enough to usually get its own way.

Where was I, oh yes, you may think that with the background Laila has, she is a pretty stuck-up girl. But she isn't. She is really down to earth, like me. We have a lot in common. We both love to party, neither of us is really into a formal relationship -- just spur of the moment stuff, we don't have any special talent, compared to the other students at the school, and we are both lots of fun. All in all, I think she's a girl you would not approve of, mom. But I think I like her. Isn't that weird, just a couple of letters ago I wanted to go home ASAP, and wanted nothing but one-night-stands, but look at me. See what one woman can do. Sheeesh!

Remember a little while back when you asked me if I needed any help with money? Does that offer still stand? I discovered I could really use the help. I'm not gonna say how much, that's up to you. Just make sure it's over $3 OK. Thanks. Oh, and while we are on the subject, I could also use some new shoes (10 ½, Nike or Adidas; white, grey or black) and a Sam Kinison tape. God, I feel like an asshole, like a beggar. You guessed it. Dad hasn't send me any money. That is his choice, but it was money I had counted on.

Oh, I called Sam. I talked for about ten minutes, then he called back for about 30 minutes. It was cool, we swapped girl stories, and we got the Europe trip straightened out. He wants to come out here, but he is really interested in a girl. I told him we didn't have to go backpacking in Europe if he can't afford it (I probably won't be able to afford it either). We can just stay here in Denmark and party, maybe visit a country, or two, or three. He will probably call you to find out about a passport and the like. I know there is still a possibility that he won't come. So I

Letter 18 – Grades

won't be crushed if he doesn't. I just think it would be really neat to see him out here, and it would also be good for him, since he has never been overseas. He sounded pretty enthusiastic when I told him about all the parties and stuff, and he's all for the backpacking idea. Either way, I'm probably gonna be here until July sometime, and I will not go up to visit your family in Sweden without you. Oh yeah, and I'll try to visit your dad in the spring, OK.

Well, my beard is back and everything is going great, for now anyway. I still miss you though. God, I wish you could fly out for a week or so, that would be so great!! Judging by how strange it was to see Nila again, I can't imagine how it would be to see you again - Mom. Just think how much I have changed, weird isn't it. Well, we knew that would happen when I came out here, right? Remember how speechless I was just after two weeks in Japan. I bet this time will be worse than back then. Still, the day I see you again is the day I look very much forward to. WOW, I've been writing for a couple of hours now and my hand hurts. I love you, write back again soon, OK.

I love you, bye Peter

P.S. My wisdom teeth are coming in, it doesn't hurt, and I just feel wiser!?!

I was happy Peter decided to attend Community College. When he graduated from high school, he had been awarded a full scholarship to one of the local Community Colleges. It also seemed like a good choice to live close to home after his year abroad.

Adolescent Abroad

In his letter Peter wrote: "everything is going great, for now anyway." He had learned that his mood changed rapidly depending on external circumstances, such as getting sick, doing poorly in school, or falling in love.

Letter 19 – A Girlfriend...

The old saying, "After darkness comes sunshine," surely applied to Peter's life in Denmark. Spring was in the air, the days were getting longer, and Peter's attitude was improving. His best friend, Sam, whom Peter has made several references to, was planning to visit him in Denmark! Sam was a fine young man who had experienced the hard knocks of life at an early age. He was an only child, living with his mother in a single-parent household. He had worked several part time jobs during high school to help his mother financially. He was responsible and well behaved. Now he had an opportunity to do something fun for himself. He was excited about his upcoming trip and frequently called me to talk about it.

In this letter, Peter mentioned that he probably has a "girlfriend." The other girlfriend he refers to was a girl he dated in eighth grade. She was very possessive of him and became angry when he spent time with his buddies rather than her. The relationship lasted about two weeks and that was the end of Peter's dating experience until his Danish spring fling.

February 4

Dear Mom.

Well, it's another Sunday and time for a weekly report. There are two stories this week.

Adolescent Abroad

Story number one - SAM'S COMING TO VISIT!!!! He called and told me he has already made the reservation and was on his way to getting a passport. He'll be staying here from June 5th until June 26th. We are going to have such a good time. He'll be here for the Big Graduation Party, so I know he's gonna have a good time. I'm all excited about that, only five more months!!! I'm still probably not heading back until July sometime.

Story number two. I've got a girlfriend, I think. Yes, it's Laila. This weekend, the whole gang went to a pub (sounds familiar), and Laila and I were already drunk by the time we got there. We talked about - US - and got to know each other a lot better, and we were kissin' the whole time. That was fun. God, it has been five years since I have gone out with someone, that is almost a quarter of my life, wait that's more than a quarter of my life. The good thing is she's not possessive like the other one. Unfortunately, I sort of am. I'll let you know how everything goes, OK.

This weekend we also saw "Dead Poets Society." It was really good. Laila and I were snuggling the whole time. That was even better. This Monday she wants to help me go grocery shopping, so I start eating right. I just finished cleaning my room, so I think I'll invite her to my place and help me put the groceries in the "fridge" (good plan?).

We're all still iffy on the trip to Cypress. It's gonna be pretty expensive. But you were wondering what we are going to do for the February break, right? Well, we are going to Sweden for a day to mess around, since they have a "Pizza Hut" over there and Denmark doesn't. It is still up in the air whether we are going to Germany; we'll see. I'll send you postcards if I do.

Letter 19 – A Girlfriend...

Sam called and told me about his girl situation. He said: "Peter, when it rains, it pours." That means, now that he has a girlfriend, other girls are starting to like him. Naturally, I felt sorry for the poor guy, but then this week I discovered that three other chicks, besides Laila, sort of have the hots for me. Chick #1 is named Nina. She is not from my school, but she recently had a party and took a liking to me. She's Dutch, but is from South Africa. Pretty good looking too. Chick #2 is Mona. She is real cute, but really small and her dad is a school principal. Chick # 3 is Gunilla from Germany. She is a combination of cuteness (because she is small), good looks (because she is), innocence (because she acts that way), and sweetness. But what do I care, I already have Laila, so I'm not so excited about it.

I'm way out of practice with girls, and these good ol' inferiority complexes won't leave me. I keep thinking I am being set up for some major humiliating experience. As a matter of fact, while we were drunk this weekend and we started to talk real well, I asked Laila: "Why me?" She said because I am really sweet, lots of fun, not fake and full of bull, like most of the other guys in school. She sounded real sincere, and I remember I was smiling my ass off. It felt nice to have someone (female) tell me they like me, and point out all my good qualities. But for some reason I just can't believe it, and I'm constantly looking for a reason to doubt what she says, this is not good. You don't have to be a shrink to know that this is a problem. Hell, if this keeps up, I may never get married and have kids, shit!

I'm thinking the reason I feel so insecure is because I'm much more vulnerable out here; away from home, family, and everything I know. I can count on that something goes wrong, so I am not letting myself get into a position where I can get squashed. Does this make sense? Please, give me some advise, OK.

I better get on with my homework. I'm doing real good in the homework department now that I have an organizer. So hopefully, we'll see some improvement on the next report card. Write back real soon. I wish I could call, because your advice probably won't come fast enough. I love you. Bye.

Love Peter

Nila gave Peter a fancy organizer for Christmas. It consisted of a large note book with dividers that separated class notes by subject matter. Each section had a different color. For example, the history notes were written on green paper, the math notes were on white. Peter humorously attributed his progress in school to that organizer.

Peter was feeling better about himself and had a good time "hanging out" with his friends during the February break. It may sound strange that they went to a different country for pizza, but a boat trip from Copenhagen to Sweden is cheap and takes only about one hour. Many people traveled that route daily. There now is a bridge between the two countries, serving people living in Sweden and working in Denmark, and vice versa.

Dating was a new and frightening experience for Peter, and he wanted my advice on how to handle his anxiety. I welcomed Peter's request for advice, and hoped that by

Letter 19 – A Girlfriend...

dealing with his concerns together, we could learn how to resolve them.

Letter 20 – ...A Break-up

Peter's dating experience with Laila was short lived. By now they had broken up, and Peter's view of women was tarnished for the rest of his stay in Denmark. When I later asked him what went wrong in the relationship, he said that Laila was unable to be a one-man-woman, and the "chemistry" between them was wrong.

February 18

Dear Mom.

Boy, it has been a while since you've heard from me, hasn't it? My winter vacation is coming to a close. You are probably wondering why I haven't written if I've had so much free time. Well, it has been an eventful week, let me tell you.

First of all, thank you for your letter, it was very comforting to hear stuff like that, but more on that later. Let me give you a summary of the week's events.

FRIDAY – was shitty. That was the night Laila and I broke up. This set the stage for all the other stuff that would happen. It was also the night I called Nila. I was feeling pretty bad, like my heart was taken out with a chainsaw to be exact. Jess was also pissed because Sean started making out with Jenny, the girl Jess was after, and Laila's best friend. Oh, and Sean was very aware that Jess was after Jenny.

SATURDAY – I woke up and went to Jess' house way out in Karlslund. Two other guys were there. One of them I went to

Spain with last fall, and I hadn't seen him since then, so it was good to meet him again and to party with some different company. By this time, Jess and Sean's friendship were pretty much kaput. Anyway, Jess and I get smashed.......wait SMASHED. That's more like it, and of course were bitching about our heartbreaks. Sean came over, and we went to a discotheque with two chicks and five guys, bad situation. Jess, Sean, and I went to the bathroom and tried settling the problem between them, but instead we became Blood Brothers. Of course I got the deepest cut and my thumb was just gushing blood. Fortunately, there was a paramedic there who fixed the thumb as best he could. One of our friends got kicked out of the place by the bouncer for being a nuisance, and we all decided to leave. I went home.

SUNDAY – well, Denmark is a small country, and of course by now Laila had heard all about my wallowing in self-petty, and how I never wanted to see her and all kinds of other false shit. So she called up early in the day and we decided to go into town and just talk, just the two of us. Boy, did we talk. She told me how her friend had bitched her out, and her mom, yes her mom, made her cry and leave the dinner table just because she dumped me. She said that Jenny had told her to keep going out with me, even if she didn't love (what a word) me. But Laila couldn't hurt me like that. She even admitted that I was too good of a guy to be going out with her, because she would end up hurting me bad (thanks for the warning). I told my side too. God, it was great. We were so afraid of each other, just shaking as we spoke about this stuff. She bought me dinner and a bunch of beers. We met Jess, Sean, Jenny and two other guys in the evening. We went to a pub, where Laila got blasted, and we

Letter 20 – ...A Break-up

played TRUTH OR DARE. Well, I was dared to kiss Laila, and we kissed for the longest time (I liked that). I guess it was a good bye kiss, because we both knew we didn't want a relationship anymore. Of course I still had feelings for her.

MONDAY – what a day that was. We spend the day with Moris, the guy who hates Laila and her friends, but is still great friends with Jess, Sean, and myself. Jess wouldn't talk to Sean, and Sean was completely blasted out of his mind and finally left the room totally pissed, but we all laughed. About five minutes later I went into the kitchen to get some more beers for everyone. Guess what I saw when I got in there. Sean was standing in the kitchen window getting ready to jump, (keep in mind we were on the third floor, and below the window is concrete, so if he didn't die, he'd at least break half the bones in his body). I snuck up on him and pulled him inside, he was resisting like an asshole, but I finally threw him into the kitchen, knocked him down, and screamed to him that if he ever did that again, I would kick the shit out of him so bad that he wouldn't be able to end his life. God, I was so pissed. He started crying his eyes out even before I started yelling at him, so I had to lighten up a little. We talked for about 45 minutes. Boy, does that kid have some problems. I knew he did though, because he is an artist. Those people are screwed in their head. I really question my friendship with him now. Anyway, I was giving him the best advice and guidance I knew how to give. I'm not a shrink, what do you want me to do, and he kept asking me how I could be so strong inside. I was kind of flattered, but in no mood to thank him. We all went to bed shortly after that, and we have had no problems with him since then. God, what a jerk, how could he think of doing something like that. I keep thinking I am taking the situation too lightly, but what am I supposed to do. Boy, and you thought your Mondays were bad. Sheesh!

TUESDAY – Jess, Sean, Laila, Jenny and I went out again. There was absolutely no communication between Laila and myself. Sean and Jenny were making out, and we decided to call it a night.

WAIT...one more thing about Monday. Moris and I were talking, and I found out why he and Laila hate each other. Sometime last year when Moris and Nisbeth, his present girlfriend were just starting to go out, Laila was in love, there is that word again, with Moris. So at a party at Moris' house, while Nisbeth was away in Sweden, Moris went into the bathroom and Laila followed. To make a long story short, they did it. This of course made me feel like shit, since I did not have sex with her, AAAARRGGG!!! Anyway, that almost ruined things between Moris and Nisbeth, and Moris takes part of the responsibility, but Nisbeth is pretty much the reason the school is split. Anyway, part of me is thinking: "what a slut Laila is," another part of me is thinking: "big deal, don't be such a hypocrite, you wish she would have done the same thing with you."

TUESDAY (cont.) – Jess spent the night at my house. Anja was being a bitch. Jess and I began talking about these chicks that screw everything up for us. I told him that I wish I knew something worse about Laila than what Moris told me, so I could get her out of my life and go on with business as usual. (See, I still like her, which is why she is driving me up the wall). Jess finally told me that Sunday night (remember the night I felt so close to Laila and so happy about our talk) when I

Letter 20 – ...A Break-up

went to the restroom, she started kissing another guy. I WENT NUTS! I felt like everything she had told me was complete bull shit. The way I figured it, she must have known that I was gonna find out sooner or later, so she must have done it just to get me out of her life. GOD, I WAS PISSED!!! Jess tried calming me down by telling me that she was drunk, and for all he knew, it could have been the guy who started it; besides, with drunk girls, all you have to do is make the first move, and you'll at least get a good kiss out of them. That is true.

WEDNESDAY – we said to heck with the chicks. Jess and I rode into town and met Sean, Gudrun, and a couple of other people from the school. I hadn't seen Gudrun since last Friday at school. She has a boyfriend now, but she says she still can't talk to him like she can talk to me. I'm happy for her though. In many ways Gudrun and I are best friends. See, when I talk to Jess and Sean, I have to put a "ring of Macho" into everything I say, but not with Gudrun. So I told her everything I told you up to this point and she consoled me. I was so glad I got to talk to her. The problem with her is that I am not physically attracted to her, so I lose again. I spent that night at Jess'.

THURSDAY – we all bought a bunch of beer, discovered a beautiful park at Osterport, bought a frisbee, and played. I got a little drunk, and we all had a great time, except Jess. Sean and Jenny were at it again. The best part was when Laila went into the bushes to pee, I followed and waited nearby in a little gazebo. When she finished she saw me and came to sit next to me. I know how hard it is to get her to talk, with her heart, instead of her head, so I started out by saying: "Laila, you play me for such a fool, but I know a lot more than you think I do."

She turned white and said: "What do you mean?" I told her about her and Moris. Boy, did she have a lot to say about that. She asked me if Moris had told me how he had bragged to everyone in the school about their little affair, and how he told her that he was gonna dump his girlfriend for her, and how she was so crazy about him, but by the end of the week, she was considered a slut by everyone and laughed at, and all that stuff. I was thinking, GULP! No, he left that part out - thanks Moris. Whew, I felt like a jerk, I remember she had told me some time ago, that one day she would tell me why she and Moris hated each other. Then, I asked her about the guy she kissed when I was with her, and I told her what I thought her motive was. She apologized over and over again, and said it was just a big mistake. Of course I believed her, but that's the kind of gullible dumb shit person I am. Well, I no longer want to go out with her, I wouldn't mind having sex with her though, and I think we will before the end of the school year. We have a weird kind of relationship. Every time I look her in the eyes, I think I can see that she regrets letting me go, and that she does think I am "just a great guy." That's what she tells all my friends anyway. I have to remember she is young (16) and has a lot of changing coming up. Remember when I was 16? I was at Lana's every day playing with toys and D&D [*Dungeons & Dragons*]. I had no social life worth mentioning. Boy, have I changed in two years. Don't worry, I am not waiting around two years for this chick, but I think somehow she'll pull through. She has a real good, loving, and caring family, a pretty good head on her shoulders, and she thinks a lot like me with the exception of a few subjects. Right now she is just too much into having a good time. We went out to dinner tonight, and everything went well.

Letter 20 – ...A Break-up

We are starting to treat each other like real people again, instead of all this game-playing bullshit. So you don't have to hate her if I don't, OK.

Onto other things. Thanks for all the kind words about me and my communication skills. Boy, you won't give up on this diplomat stuff, will you. Did you know, out of some 5,000 people who attend Foreign Services school, only ten get a job in the field. Scary, huh? I am looking for a profession where I have a better chance of getting work than in that field, 500 to 1 doesn't look good to me. I can't go to school for a long time and not be able to get the job I want with the Foreign Services. That would piss me off. Did you know that the best way to get a job in the Foreign Services, is to go into the military?

My money situation sucks, I'm gonna ask the school if they can lower my tuition, so I have more money for myself. I live cheaply, I even buy cheap beer, but I am still struggling. No, dad hasn't send me any money yet. Oh remember, how I asked you for shoes a while back? I wasn't kidding, my shoes look like shit now. Guess it is the damp weather that is so hard on the shoes. Please, hurry!.

Health great! School great as well. I feel like I'm really putting more effort into studying, so hopefully, it will show on the next report card.

Girls! Hate 'em but love 'em. I don't think I'll ever get married, because I always fall for the same type of chick. Susan, juggling like four guys. Ann, already had a boyfriend. In other words, I always go for those chicks that I know it could never work out with. I must be messed up in my head. Beer is the only thing I trust, and Nila and you of course. God, this sucks, the more I think about it, the more I think I am due for a life of loneliness. YUCK! Oh, and all the talk about another chick coming around, forget it. Remember, there are only 100 students in this school, half of which are girls, five of which are semi-attractive, three of which are taken, one of which is like a sister (Pina), and the one left just dumped me. AAAAHHHHHH!!!!! Someone kill me!!!! God, I hate this part of being here.

I'm having a great time, except for the girl part. The weather is beautiful, warm, sunny, springtime, flowers blooming. What more can I ask for besides money, shoes, and a GIRL!!!

Well, that is all for now. I love you and can't wait to get back home, where I will surely go through the same game-playing again and again. I miss you.

Love Peter

P.S. You have seen the happy, sad, confused, drunk, studly, stern, and mean Viking. May I introduce the insane one. Tadaa!

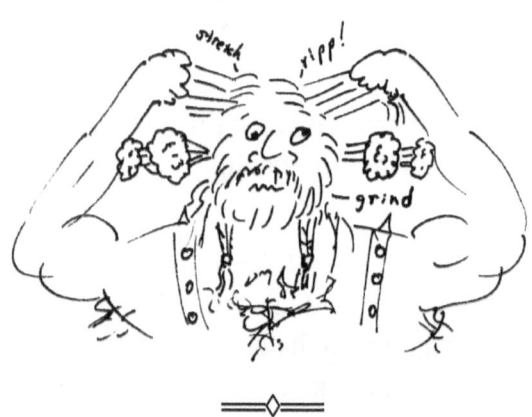

Letter 20 – ...A Break-up

The break-up with Laila disappointed Peter, and the tension between his two best friends, Jess and Sean, added to his frustration. Jess and Sean were both in love with the same girl, and on several occasions Peter tried to mediate between them. Becoming Blood Brothers, an old Viking tradition, seemed to be the perfect way to resolve the problem once and for all. According to this custom, Blood Brothers swear loyalty to each other for life. Peter had studied Viking history since he was a little boy and was familiar with the tradition. He was proud of being a descendent of the old Vikings and becoming a Blood Brother strengthened his Viking image.

Peter finally lost patience with Sean, when he reacted so dramatically to his problems with Jess. Years earlier, two of Peter's class mates had committed suicide. The first incident happened while Peter was in Middle School. A young boy shot himself. Two years later another bright and sensitive high school student committed suicide. These incidents devastated Peter, and he wanted to use all his psychological "know-how" to help prevent Sean from making such an irreversible mistake.

Although male-bonding was important for Peter, the most meaningful relationship was between he and Gudrun. She became the one in whom Peter confided, and they developed a lasting friendship. In contrast, Laila soon disappeared from Peter's circle of friends.

Letter 21 – Things on My Mind

A Danish gymnasium is a school similar to a community college in the U.S. It is not associated with sports. All students pursuing a higher education must attend gymnasium for three years before entering a university. In this letter Peter elaborated on a party he and his friends attended at Ordrup Gymnasium. Ordrup is a middle to upper class suburb north of Copenhagen. The trains go from Copenhagen Central station to Ordrup station several times an hour. Peter had a transit card that allowed him to ride buses and trains in Copenhagen and its suburbs. A transit card is cheap, and riding trains and buses is comfortable and widespread in Denmark.

March 4

Dear Mom.

Here goes another weekly report. God, I feel bad about not writing as much as I used to. I've got a lot on my mind. Actually, I've only four things on my mind: Laila, money, and summer, oh yes, and school. But that occupies a lot of my time, so I usually only write on Sunday afternoons now. Sorry about the graph paper, but I forgot to bring my regular notebook home, so I have to improvise.

OK, not much happened this week. Laila and I are playing the guessing game with each other...still. God, it sucks, we have been reduced to teasing each other now. You know, a slap here, a pinch there, a tickle, or a push down the stairs, really getting out some of that sexual frustration. It's so irritating.

Then, I found out about a party being held by one of my friends who hates Laila and company, and guess what? Sean and I were not invited. That didn't bother Sean, since he had been sick and out of school all week, but it hurt my feelings. They hold it against me, that I'm trying to get a girlfriend, or something like that. What am I supposed to do, drop my interest in Laila and go "jerk off" at their parties. God, I was pissed off.

Anyway, Jess didn't go to the party either since I wasn't invited, so instead we went to a party at Ordrup Gymnasium. There were a lot of strange characters at the party, and Laila was there too. She came over to me and started bugging me about why I hadn't called Sean this week. That pissed me off too, and for the first time I raised my voice to her. I felt bad though, because I could see in her face that she knew I was slipping out of her grasp.

I decided to leave early with some friends. When we were outside, one of the girls came running after me to tell me that some guy was starting trouble with Jess, because he was hitting on one of the good looking chicks. I said "WHAT!" and headed back to the dance with one other guy. I really wanted to "kick some ass," and for the first time in a while my mind was free from my thoughts of Laila, so I decided to stick with that state of mind.

When I got inside, I asked Jess who the guy was that gave him trouble, so I could tell him to mind his own business. But Jess would not tell me, so I hung around anyway. One of the guys

Letter 21 – Things on My Mind

there was so deliriously drunk that he couldn't stand and was puking everywhere. One of the chaperones asked me to throw him out of the building, and I did. That wasn't nice of me. Then the party ended, and all kinds of fights started. I broke one up by myself. Then, a few minutes later a guy started yelling at me, telling me to let them fight. I told him to mind his own business. So he pushed me, and I pushed him back so hard that he flew away (I was impressed by myself, but my hands hurt a lot, because they were freezing in the cold weather). A couple of his friends helped him up and calmed him down, while my friends pulled me back.

Once I calmed down, Laila tried talking me into leaving with her, but I pulled my hand away from hers and told her to go ahead. Now she really felt like shit, and I felt sorry for her, but there was so much action going on, that I didn't want to let it go to waste by going with her to play more games.

Saturday I went to school to wait for Jess to finish his ACT test and I found out that Laila was there too developing film. So I went to the physics lab, which is also the dark room, to say "Hi." After a while her friends left us alone, but we could not say a thing to each other, just a little small-talk and a little teasing. I even did a few physics experiments to show off my intelligence; she laughed. Anyway, we were right back to normal again, no damage had been done from the previous night, I hope. She had to babysit that evening, so my friends and I went to see a movie called "Born on the Fourth of July." It was a sad movie. I don't think I'll volunteer for any war, that's for sure. That was it for this week.

Adolescent Abroad

Can you tell me for sure if Nila coming out here this summer? If she doesn't come I'll try to catch the same flight home as Sam, OK.

From what I hear, Sam and his girlfriend broke up. And Mom, how come you tell me that she is a "plain Jane" when my other friends, like Juan and Sam tell me she is hot? I guess you have a different taste, which means you will probably not like Laila, besides, she smokes, too. She tried talking me into helping her quit, but I refused.

We can forget about having me fly back through Singapore and Japan. I don't know how we can afford it. I talked the school into lowering my tuition for now, then when you come, you can pay the rest, is that OK with you. I'll pay you back when I start working. I can't wait till you come here, only 89 days left. How are you and Nila and Shadow? All good I hope.

I talked to an old friend of mine from high school, who is going to an in-state university. She's moving to Colorado by herself next semester and going to a community college until she establishes residency there, then she will go to the University of Colorado at Boulder. This way she does not have to pay all the out-of-state tuition. Pretty good plan, eh. I wonder if I should do something like that.

I took a few pictures of my pad so you can see what you are about to visit. I'm not sending any pictures of Laila until I get a really good one. I showed her some pictures of Nila; she thinks Nila is gorgeous. She almost died when I told her Nila is only 15 years old. Jess and Sean want copies of Nila's pictures.

Letter 21 – Things on My Mind

Well, that is it for this week. Pretty uneventful, only four pages. I miss you so much. Write soon, ok. I love you.

Love Peter

P.S. I talked to some people who went to the party I wasn't invited to, and they said it sucked royally. That's what happens when the BEAST isn't around to liven things up.

Peter had never been a fighter, and his behavior at the party in Ordrup was out of character. I was not surprised, however. His frustration was apparent in his letters.

Peter and his friends saw "Born on the Fourth of July," about a paralyzed Vietnam veteran who became an anti-war spokesman back in the States. Peter was impressed with Tom Cruise's performance and enjoyed the movie.

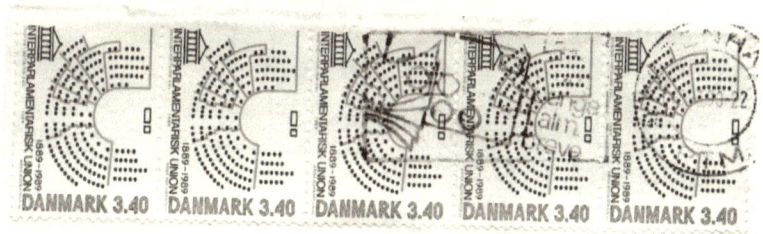

Letter 22 – Winter Lingers

Peter appeared energetic and lighthearted around his friends. He livened up parties and offered emotional support when needed. In turn he was respected for his strength and apparent self confidence. I believed that his letters were very therapeutic and helped Peter be strong and cheerful around friends.

March 7

Dear Mom.

Surprise! This is the first time in a long time I've written more than one letter in a week. I made the mistake of taking a nap after school today, without setting my alarm. Now I'm wide awake, it's almost midnight, and I'm gonna be dead tired tomorrow. I miss you! I sometimes wish I had someone around to make sure I don't sleep through the alarm clock in the morning. I do that a lot. What I am saying, is that I always wish that. God, I sure make a lot of mistakes out here. It's a wonder I'm still alive and kicking. Don't worry so much about me. Even though I sound bummed in my letters and on the phone, I'm still doing pretty well.

Everyone is getting sick out here. There is almost a new epidemic every week, and Anja catches all of them. All my schoolmates are home sick. Sean has been sick for seven days now, and will probably stay home for three more days. Laila is sick too, and Jess is getting a sore throat, so he'll probably be out before the week is out. I got a sore throat about three epidemics ago, but I only stayed home one day, then it was gone. Guess I'm just a healthy kinda guy. At least I know I don't have AIDS or something, since I still haven't had sex.

Last Sunday after I wrote you, I decided I'd like to hear Dad's voice. So I called him up, another mistake, all he did was talk business (I was stupid for expecting otherwise). Needless to say, the conversation did not go well, and I felt like a real idiot after the conversation was over. Well, he's my dad (thanks Mom). Sooooorryyyyyyyy!

Well, the weather is lousy out here, and of course everyone's attitude is affected by it. Did you know, everybody from school I've talked to hates the school, the classes, the teachers, the lack of courses, and the lousy teaching methods. Everyone is in a kind of "don't care" state of mind. But they're all glad they came, because of the friends they made, the parties, and the pubs.

God, I feel sorry for all of them, they are so mixed up. They know that they might have to move to a different country in the next year or so, so they make as many close friends as they can in their travels. I think this is why they all get more "action" (sex) than I do. God, that sucks! You can tell, this is driving me up the wall. By the way, your "girl" advice sucks. How am I suppose to get an older girl to go out with me, when younger ones don't even want to. AHHHHGGG! I give up.

Let's see what else has happened. Monday and Tuesday - nothing. Today, I got the highest grade on a math test that I've gotten this year, an amazing 63%, so you can imagine how bad the others were. Well, are you convinced I've completely lost

Letter 22 – Winter Lingers

my mind? And somehow I manage to get "C's" in the class. Cool grading system, huh. Actually, the teacher is just glad I don't drop into the lower math class. Instead I stick this out no matter how much I fail. Ha Ha!! Story of my life, I know it is a neat character trait, but dammit, I don't know how much longer I can take it, I gotta start winning soon. I don't see any light at the end of this tunnel either, just more and more failures. I can't wait til June, so I don't have to worry about how much it costs you and me out here.

I think the bank screwed up because I am missing 300 Kr. Actually, my heart is beating like a drum, because I can't afford to loose 20 Kr. I am looking into it tomorrow. See, I have one of those day-and-night teller cards, and I think someone else is sharing my account. I am having a hard time with money. Everything is so expensive out here. I had a bowl of rice for dinner. If it is good enough for the Chinese, it is good enough for me.

Oh yes, Anja rented "Beaches" with Bette Midler, God, what a great movie. I cried. At least my taste in movies are improving, but sorry, "Accidental Tourist" is still on the bottom of my "Good Movies I have seen" list.

I better go to bed now, it's 1:00 in the morning. I love you. Write me a long good letter that I can sink my teeth into, Ok. I go through those postcards in about three seconds. I miss you so much. Bye.

Love Peter

P.S. If you win the lottery, don't decide to keep it a secret and surprise me when I get back. OK. Luv ya'

Adolescent Abroad

Peter's friendships were based on conversations and exchange of ideas rather than action, such as sex, and he made deep and lasting relationships with males as well as females. Unfortunately, Peter thought "scoring" with girls to be much more masculine that developing meaningful relationships. His failure to "score" had been grating on him since high school. Peter felt resentment when the jocks referred to him as a nerd because he was not part of the party scene, where sex and drugs were common. No matter how hard I tried to reassure Peter that he was as masculine as the jocks, he still saw himself as inferior to them.

When Peter began socializing with rich students in Denmark, his feelings of inferiority worsened. He had enough money to live comfortably there. However, his budget did not include many extravagant expenses, such as eating out, frequent partying, and traveling. In addition, Peter's feelings of inferiority were exacerbated by his academic deficiencies.

When I enrolled Peter in the Danish school, I did not foresee these problems. Extravagant living and sexual pressures were not part of the Danish culture I grew up in. I empathized with Peter and helped him as much as I could both financially and emotionally. I realized that "poverty" was easier to cope with among loving kin, but in unfamiliar surroundings money could at least buy short-term happiness.

Letter 23 – Pick-Pocket

I occasionally sent Peter a big "care" package with his favorite cereal, snacks, shampoo, soap, and other things he liked. The boxes would go by ship and take five to eight weeks to arrive at Peter's door. Nila brought a big box of goodies when she visited for Christmas, now the arrival of another box was pending. I enjoyed getting those packages together for Peter, and I knew he appreciated them very much.

When Peter and Nila were growing up, we saved our money for small trips. For example, we always planned a trip to the Zoo for spring break, and enjoyed a picnic in the beautiful surroundings. In the summers we traveled to a lake or the mountains, and every three to four years we went to Europe. For fall break, we drove to a forest to see the beautiful colors, and in winters we went skiing, and made trips to the mountains to cut a Christmas tree. Peter was reminiscing about the fun we had on our trips and wished he could go with Nila and I on our upcoming spring trip.

March 19

Dear Mom.

I just got your packet today. YEAH! I went through the Granola bars in about 5 seconds, the pudding and half the Reese cups are being saved for later, and the shoes fit great. Thank you. You know what is weird? I had a feeling, a strong feeling, that I was gonna get some mail today; after about a week of no mail. It sounds like you have a wonderful Spring break planned with Nila. I wish I could go too. Boy, you guys are seeing all kinds of places while I'm gone. I'm jealous. Me, I won't be going anywhere for Spring break. I've gotten another phone bill to brace myself for.

Just ten more weeks till school is over, and you and Sam will be here. I can't wait. Those ten weeks are gonna ZOOM by so quickly, now that spring is here. It was 72 degrees today. Heck, it was only ten weeks since Laila and I met, and that seems like yesterday now. By the way, we are doing terrible.

It won't be long now and I'll be home. Make sure to tell me if Nila is coming out, because my "take-off" date depends on that.

I felt much better after I talked to you last Friday. I guess I talked pretty loud, because I woke up Anja, and she heard everything I said, and of course made fun of me the next day when I asked her for an aspirin. That's weird, when I drink with friends I can have a great time, but I guess when I had a few beers alone, it can hit me the wrong way. Whew, I hope that never happens again. I told Jess and Sean about it a couple of days later, and they both said they have had that same experience lots of times.

Jess and Sean are still fighting, but Sean broke up with Anna, so it looks like things might start patching themselves up in time for spring and summer. Good, I hope so.

Latest news... I can't remember if I told you about the "pick-pocket" I tangled with, let me know.

Letter 23 – Pick-Pocket

Today I had a huge test on China from 1900 to Tienanmen Square. I think I did pretty well. I'm like a China expert now. You are not gonna believe this, but I side with the Commies, at least until last June. But "Chinese Reds" only, NO Soviets.

I don't know what's been happening in the world the last couple of months, since I quit buying Time magazine. Too expensive. I'll catch up on the recent history later when it is ancient.

Well, it's past my bedtime, again. I love you, as always. Write soon.

Love Peter

Peter learned a very important lesson that Friday evening when he drank beers alone in his room. He had been depressed and the drinking exacerbated his depression. He called home that evening and we talked for a while until he felt better.

During the conversation he told me about being pick-pocketed one morning when he met his friends in a coffee house before school started. While he was sitting at the table talking and enjoying his coffee and a pastry, he felt something pushing at his back pocket. He quickly turned around and caught a young man with his wallet. Peter immediately grabbed the guy and threatened to beat him up. The guy threw the wallet on the floor and Peter let him go. Peter felt like a hero after that incident.

Copenhagen is a very cosmopolitan city with many coffee houses and pubs. Peter enjoyed sitting around in those old-

time places socializing and eating with his friends. Indeed, that lifestyle had become more important to him than buying *Time* magazine and reading about news from the U.S. He was usually well informed about current events, and used to spend much time reading and learning about both past and present affairs.

One recent event was the Tienanmen Square massacre, which deeply upset Peter. When he had the opportunity to study history, one of his favorite subjects, he became an "expert" on modern Chinese history. Contrary to his politics he sided with the Chinese Reds until the Tienanmen slaughter the previous June.

Letter 24 – Spring At Last

It had not been difficult for me to raise Peter and Nila. We understood the importance of being a good team; to trust, respect, and communicate with each other. Peter and Nila were a strong dyad, as well, and had a way of keeping each other in line. They supported and consoled each other. When Nila wrote Peter expressing concern about his drinking habits, he immediately reassured her that he would stop drinking as soon as he was back in the States.

In Denmark, beer drinking is common, even among teenagers. However, it is not the public hazard that it is in the States because teenagers rarely drive cars. The Danish public transportation system is excellent and is the customary way of getting around in Copenhagen. Obtaining a driver's license is a very expensive undertaking. One must enroll in a licensed driving school and practice driving many hours with a certified teacher. Also, before taking a driving test, one must pass a very difficult oral exam. Most people, therefore, do not start driving until they are in their mid-twenties.

I did not worry about Peter's drinking. I trusted that he was safe among good friends. When I sent extra money, however, I advised him to spend it on food and traveling rather than alcohol. He did not always follow my advise.

Adolescent Abroad

March 26

Dear Mom,

Thanks for your huge letter that was great. I also got your postcard and a letter from Nila. I stayed home because all my muscles are aching and I thought I might be getting the flu that is going around now. So rather than letting it get worse, so that I would have to stay out of school longer, I decided to kill it off today. But your letter just made my day. I am a little behind in my letter writing, so I think I'll spend this day catching up.

First, tell Nila not to worry about me. Doesn't she know that I am completely indestructible!! I must admit girls come the closest to finishing me off, but otherwise I'm cool. If you guys are worried about me drinking, just think in about three month I won't be allowed to drink, legally anyway, and since I am a law abiding citizen, I will straighten out. Now, do you guys feel better.

Sorry I called up crying a couple of weeks ago, but that only happens 1 in 150 times, and that was about the 150th time, so I deserved it.

Also, if I were Nila, I would think twice about going to France for a year alone. It is really a bigger test of yourself than you think. Plus it would be expensive for me, since I'd have to fly out there once a month to make sure she doesn't get in trouble. Just look at me and see how I have changed, not so good, eh. Of course it is her decision, and yours. And she being a girl and all, will probably do the exact opposite of what I advise.

Letter 24 – Spring At Last

Onto other things. I read in Newsweek, I think, that "The Hunt for Red October" stunk! Good thing all my friends in the States are telling me it is great. I should know better than to listen to these damn movie critics, or to doubt Sean Connery. Next week I am gonna see "War of the Roses" with the cast from "Romancing the Stone." I am a big Danny Devito fan. I still hold a grudge for having to see "Accidental Tourist" over "Twins," remember what a good movie the critics said that was? SHEESH!!!

Well Mom, it was a real nice conversation we had on the phone the other day. I hope I sounded happy enough so you won't worry so much about me. Jess thinks you are so cool, so do all my other friends. They can't believe I can talk to you as well as I can. They are all envious of me. Gudrun can't wait to see you.

I have a chance to go to Bornholm this weekend for the girls' last basketball game. Gudrun and Laila are both playing. It would be fun to go. We would get a cabin on the seven hour boat ride and party the whole time. You know how much I like boats. Unfortunately, it costs a lot of money, and I think it wouldn't be a good idea to use all that money. We'll see if I go.

Anja and I are getting along much better. I try to put myself in her place sometimes. I must drive her nuts, but I feel sorry for her. I hope I don't live like her in the future. She does try to give me whatever advise she can, so I appreciate that.

By the way, I guess I forgot to tell you, that a long time ago I was rearranging the furniture in my room, and changing my earring at the same time. (This is what Anja gets mad at me for, I do a hundred different things at the same time, and get none of them done). Anyway, I took out my earring and finished rearranging my room, but by that time I was so tired that I fell asleep and didn't wake up until the next day. Then I discovered that I couldn't get my new earring through the ear. I was pissed, the ear had healed over night. I guess I'm a pretty healthy guy. I meant to get the ear repierced, when suddenly I was struck by financial destruction. I kept putting it off and then I realized I could buy a whole chicken for what it costs to get the ear pierced again. I have reached the point where food comes before beauty. So don't worry about me visiting your father with an earring.

Spring is so pretty here. All the flowers are blooming, but my nose is going nuts, not half as bad though as back home.

About the spring break. Jess has an uncle that lives in Jutland, and the guy is rich. He has something like seven different houses with 26 bedrooms each, huge lots of land, factories, horses, lakes, boats, hunting areas, you name it. We were thinking about visiting him for the break.

As for Laila and I, I guess I didn't mention her, because I was trying to get her out of my thoughts. But last Friday my friends and I went to a pub together, and Laila was there too. She tried to confront me with this ignoring B.S. I didn't want to talk about it, since we were sitting at a table with ten other interested people. So we didn't. I feel like kind of a jerk, though, because I can see that it bugs her, and it bugs me, too. Besides, I really miss all the good talks we had, and being alone with her. But the problem is that I either have to love her or hate her, no in-between, because if we are just friends, I'm gonna love her, but she won't return it, and that's what hurts the most. She wants to

Letter 24 – Spring At Last

be friends, but I have to forget her for good, that's my only option. That hurts her, and I don't want that either. Why is it that for every question answered, ten new ones arise?

Onto other things. Guess what I forgot to tell you the night I called. I was invited to a strip-poker game where everyone lost. Out here the girls don't chicken out, like in the States. I suck at poker, so I didn't go. Good thing, I probably would have died with all those naked chicks around, because I am so horny these days. What a country this is. I love you and can't wait to see you in June.

Love Peter

P.S. I miss those Hawaiian bread sandwiches with roast beef that you used to make!

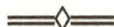

I always worried about how Peter and Anja got along. Most of the time they got along well. She later told me it had been a real eye-opening experience to house Peter. She is a loner and has no family.

Peter felt that without a family, life would not be worth living. He liked to tell his friends about his family and the close relationship we had. His friends generally thought I was cool, and considered me their friend. I was aware of the image Peter painted of me and tried hard to live up to it.

I was able to switch easily between being a parent and being a friend to my children. It was initially difficult for Peter's friends to understand that relationship. They were puzzled by my open-mindedness and wondered why I was such an easy-

going mom. I recognized early on that Peter needed to make his own decisions, and learn from his mistakes. I was, therefore, happy to learn that Peter had chosen to spend his money on food rather than re-piercing his ear. Peter had always been a "big spender." His allowance was typically spent within a few hours of receiving it, and rarely did he have the patience to save for an expensive item.

Perhaps it might be more correct to say that Peter had different priorities about how to spend his money than I thought he should have. For example, Peter had the opportunity to visit Bornholm island with a group from his school. Bornholm is a small island located to the east of Copenhagen in the Baltic Sea between Denmark and Poland. It is a very quaint and unique island. The main industry is fishing. The people catch and smoke herring for world-wide export. I had visited there as a teenager and later as an adult. One can take the night ferry from Copenhagen and arrive in Bornholm the next morning. It is a popular place to take a biking vacation. Because I had had so much fun there, I wanted Peter to go. Unfortunately, he declined the invitation; a visit to Bornholm was not as important to Peter as it was to me.

Section V. Winding down

This section holds Peter's last five letters, written between early April and mid-May. It is a beautiful time of year in Denmark. The days stretch and stretch after winter hibernation. Birds busy themselves nesting in trees, singing and dancing in the sky, welcoming spring. Tulips, daffodils, and other flowers break the barren winter ground. Trees that looked dead during the winter dress themselves in beautiful greens. Spring unfolds. Everything comes alive.

Peter is winding down, separating himself from his friends and life in Denmark. Leaving Denmark was a bitter-sweet experience. As his departure approached, Peter felt sad to be separating from his new friends.

Letter 25 – Movies

Peter probably watched more movies in Denmark than he had in his entire life. Going to the movies was never one of my priorities. I preferred traveling; museums; symphony, ballets, and theater. In this letter Peter gave me a thumbs up or down on movies he had recently seen.

April 5

Dear Mom.

Well, I guess I owe you another letter. I didn't realize how much time had gone by since my last letter. So I guess I'll let you know how the week went. First, I saw a bunch of movies:

"Rainman" with Dustin Hoffman and Tom Cruise; thumbs up.

"Farewell to the King" (I think) with Nick Nolte; OK

"Tango and Cash" with Sylvester Stallone and Kurt Russell. Stallone is getting better, but Kurt gave the movie what little it had; thumbs down.

"Gorillas in the Mist" with Sigourney Weaver; good, but something was missing.

"Tequila Sunrise" with Kurt Russell, Mel Gibson, and Michelle Pfeiffer; great crime story, total mystery, even Anja was stumped.

Finally, I saw "Twins" with Danny Devito and Arnold Schwartz~~; OK, but it didn't live up to its reputation.

Anja rented most of these movies. I rented "Gorillas" and went out to see "Tango and Cash." Gosh, I'm getting real critical of movies. They just don't make them like they used to anymore.

Speaking of movies, I don't think we have to worry about them making a movie about me and the Chickenpox, it wasn't all that exciting. I was over the sick part after about three days, the rest of the week (seven days total), was spent getting rid of the sores. I still have scabs, because I scratched like I wasn't suppose to, but scratching felt so good, and scars don't bug me, so what the heck.

You might have received my grades by now. Not bad, eh. Stayed the same in Danish, went down in Social Anthropology, but I despise that class, so it doesn't bug me, and the other classes I improved, including History, where I got an "A", finally. AAAHHH, just one quarter left.

Here is some sad news, last Monday Anja had her cat put to sleep. She was kinda sad, but seems to be in a better mood now. I kinda miss the little fella, but she was 14 years old and real sick, so I guess it was for the better.

Well, I have spring break starting tomorrow for ten days. I'll be staying in Copenhagen. I've only got two big parties planned, not my parties, just parties I plan to attend. The rest of the week I am gonna try to relax. I offered to help Anja in case she wanted any chores done, so she is puttin' the old brain to work.

That is about it; my attitude has improved. I simply don't give a shit since I'm going home soon. Do you want me to come up with an exact date so you can get a ticket? Anyway, every time I start to think of things that get me down, like girls, I just say

Letter 25 – Movies

"screw it" and I feel much better. This makes me in a much better mood, and it really shows, so I will stick with it. I miss you and love you lots!!!

Write soon, love Peter

Peter called home to tell me that he had a rash and blisters all over his body. We decided it was chicken pox, and that he needed to buy medication for the itching, then stay in bed until he felt better. This time he did not seem upset about being sick and absent from school like he had in the past.

Peter's mood was improving along with his grades. It was very important for him to do well in school. He had been an excellent student until seventh grade; then slacked off for a couple of years. In high school he regained interest in school, and graduated with honor. I never helped Peter with his schoolwork or checked his assignments; he needed to take responsibility for his student obligations.

Peter also had house chores at home. In fact, he did all our house cleaning. He did an excellent job, and considering his domestic skills, it was not out of character for Peter to offer Anja his help with spring cleaning. Nila and I missed Peter's domestic help while he was in Denmark, neither she nor I cared much for house cleaning. We both enjoyed cooking, however, and Peter greatly appreciated our good food.

Letter 26 – Happy B.D. Mom

In Denmark, Easter holiday extends over several days. Offices close, both in the public and private sector. People use the holiday to work in their garden or travel to southern Europe. Peter did not realize that Easter is an extended holiday, and was disappointed to find the post office closed when he went to mail my birthday letter.

Peter was reminiscing about my birthday celebrations, and I was recalling those past times, as well. As children Peter and Nila developed birthday and Mother's day ceremonies for me. The routine went as follows: Peter set his alarm for early morning, just before dawn. Then he woke up Nila, jumped on his bike, and rode to the nearby convent garden to cut a few beautiful roses for me. Meanwhile, Nila prepared my breakfast. Peter made a card, on which they expressed their appreciation for me. Then, they served me breakfast in bed on a tray with the flowers and the card. They were always excited when they brought their arrangement to my bedroom. I was puzzled that they developed this ceremony. I had never asked them to do anything special for me, yet they both eagerly participated in the celebration starting at a very young age.

I would lay in bed pretending to be asleep, and listen to their whispering and the gentle clanging of pots and pans in the kitchen. I felt fortunate.

Adolescent Abroad

April 13

Dear Mom.

Thanks you for all the letters. Too bad my letter writing habits aren't as good lately as yours, but I have managed to take some time this spring break to write. Yesterday, my friends and I went to Lubeck in Germany for the day. That was fun, I really love that country. I'll have to take up German again sometime. We were all talking about going there once a month, two more trips maximum. One of the guys who went with us is Danish, but he has lived in the States for many years, so he is like Jess and I. Two of the other guys are "just" Danes. They are not as wild as we are, but real cool, and just by looking at them, you know they would go to hell and back for their friends.

Otherwise there is not much to report. I got my phone bill, and I should be able to handle it, thanks to you. I have been partying a lot this week, naturally, but I have not gotten drunk, so that is good. Nothing new with Laila, things are just getting worse. I called Lisa today to wish her a happy birthday, and guess what? She is doing the same stuff I was complaining about. See, she got a boyfriend, and they are all in love, love, love. In fact, so in love that they have a joint bank account, so they can put their money together to fix his car. Then, they are going to get a joint insurance on his car, and he will teach her to drive. Then, they are moving in together and get married. Of course I said:

WHAT!!!!

I couldn't believe it. Another friend bites the dust. Maybe I'm too cynical (if misspelled say out loud). I just can't believe that it could work, but on the other hand, if it does work, I will be

Letter 26 – Happy B.D. Mom

pissed, jealous that is. God, why do these people wanna grow up so quick, what are they trying to prove, or am I wrong? AAAARRRGGG! It's so confusing, so I'll quit talking about it.

That was nice talking to you and Nila the other day, but I still can't wait to talk to you in person. I am so sorry I won't be there for your birthday, but I made a little something for you anyway. I'm sorry you won't get it on time. I didn't know Denmark closed down the three days before Easter. I hope you don't mind too much.

I can't wait to see all the new modern stuff we got at home. Figures you would get it when I am not there to hog it all. I'll bet that new Pavarotti CD sounds great. They sound so much better than tapes and records. I hear opera every time I go to Laila's house. She and her parents just love it, even I admit it sounds good, so I guess I'm changing for the better in some ways.

Let's see what else....I already told you "yes" on the Jutland idea. I haven't received your packet yet. None of the money in my account is being stolen. Tell Nila not to feel bad about learning to drive before me. Hell, it's my own fault. Oh, and as for dad giving me money, I'm not counting on it. You know how dad and I get along when it comes to money, besides, I haven't heard from him for some time.

Tell Nila good luck on her diet. I'm a little worried about her starving herself. The only times I get sick out here, is when I'm not eating (end of month), or not sleeping (heavy party weekends), and I don't want her to get sick because she is dieting. So Mom, you better watch out for that. I am so proud of her though, and how her modeling career is coming along. And I am proud of you too, Mom, for wanting to keep going to school and better yourself. Hopefully, Nila and I will learn from your example.

Well, I'll try to write more often, OK. I love you and miss you.

Love Peter

Peter enjoyed his trip to Germany and wanted to learn the German language. His academic schedule at the international school had initially included German. However, difficulties adjusting to a new culture, living on his own, and meeting the challenge of a difficult academic program caused him to drop German from his schedule.

European students learn several languages. At Peter's school in Copenhagen, most students spoke at least three. Since Peter was fluent only in English, he felt inferior to the other students.

I had empathy with Peter and always tried to brighten his days. I decided to go to his graduation, and to also attend my high school reunion. Peter was very excited when I told him I had made plans to come. We are best friends, and counted the days until we would meet again.

I suggested that he, Sam, and I take a road trip to Jutland before we went back to the States. He thought that was a great idea. It was very important for Peter to be a great host for Sam in Denmark, and I was happy to help him accomplish that task.

Letter 26 – Happy B.D. Mom

Although Peter was preoccupied with surviving in Denmark and making arrangement for Sam's visit, he still wanted to maintain contact with his other friends back home. Part of doing that was to remember everyone's birthday. When he called Lisa on her birthday and learned about her 'boyfriend situation' he was upset. Lisa was one of Peter's high school buddies, an only child living with her mother. She had never dated, and Peter was worried about her sudden decision to become seriously involved with her first boyfriend.

Peter had difficulties with authority and control. He often asked me for advice, but did not want me to tell him what to do. I knew he had to make his own mistakes in life, then suffer the consequences; I hoped they would not be too severe. Apart from the emotional pain he experienced in Denmark, he also encountered some practical problems, such as mismanaging money. In an earlier letter, Peter expressed concern that someone else might have taken money out of his account. He had since learned that only he had done so, and that he needed to be more careful with his money. It was a good lesson for him to learn.

Peter had inner conflicts about growing up. On one hand, he wanted to be very independent, on the other, he was not in a hurry to become an adult. For example, Nila had obtained her driver's license as soon as she turned sixteen, but Peter was still without a license at eighteen. Peter practiced driving when he was fifteen, but a close friend had a serious accident and Peter lost interest. Realizing the danger of having a spirited young male behind the wheel, I was happy, but still dreaded the day when he would start to drive.

Adolescent Abroad

One aspect of maturation is to outgrow one's self-centeredness and show concern for others. In that respect Peter was very mature. In spite of all his problems in Denmark, he was never so wrapped up in himself that he was inattentive to others. He expressed concern about Nila's dieting habits. She was modeling and struggled to meet the body requirements.

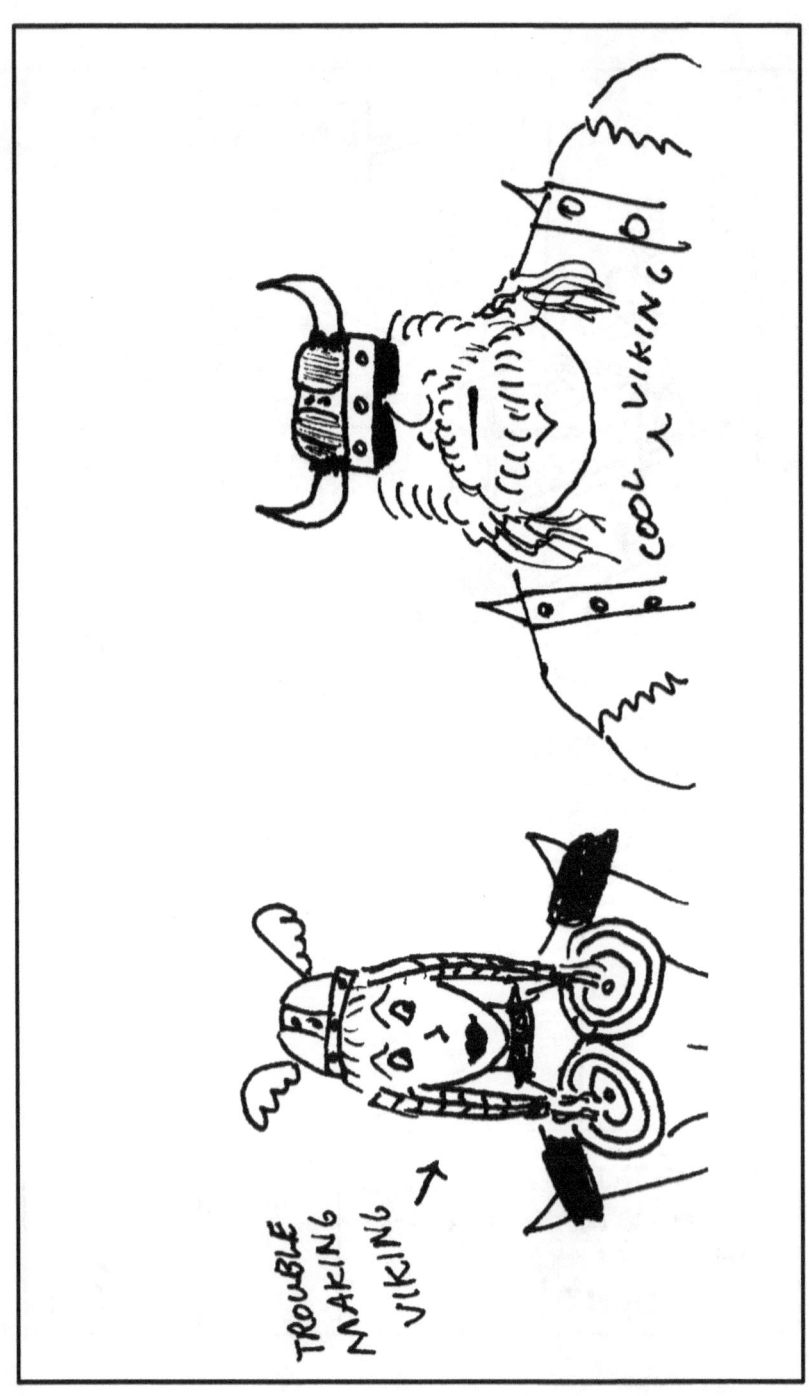

Letter 27 – Male Bonding

Peter was winding down in Denmark. His letters became short and less frequent. He lost interest in girls and cut back on partying and drinking. I was happy to learn that Peter was separating himself from his Danish life. Leaving would then be much easier.

April 22

Dear Mom,

Well, it is time for another one of my weekly reports. By the way, I only have five more to write until you get out here, Mom. Gosh, that is nothing. I was gonna call you tonight, but I decided to slow down on the long distance phone calls, since I called all my friends and you during my spring break, except Pia. I tried calling her twice, but once I got her dad, and the answering machine the second time. It costs about $10 each time just to connect with the US, and $5 each minute after that, so I decided twice was enough.

Everything is back to normal out here, aside from the fact that I am thinking about kicking Sean's ass! He hasn't done anything to me, I don't think he would dare, but he steps all over everyone else, all of my friends. Oh yeah, and he is a complete wimp. Let me explain. See all of us guys out here rely on male bonding. That means, we are all buddies to the end, and we'll warn each other if a girl is about to screw things up between the rest of us guys, like Anna, the girl who screwed things up between Sean, Jess and I. Women don't have anything like this, that's why this male bonding is so neat. You women always work against each other. Anyway, we all agreed that Anna was trouble, and that we should stay away from her, even if she is the best looking girl in the school. Sean agreed to this too, but... the minute we turned our backs to him, he was hitting on her again, what a spineless wimp. The rest of us have turned down opportunities to get laid, because of our friends, and that is a good feeling. It reassures us, that we are not slaves to our balls. Basically, Sean has made about 20 promises like that, and he has broken them all regardless of who it hurts. Well, does it sound like I should kick his ass?

I only got drunk once this week, and that wasn't even bad, it was more like a strong buzz. See...I'm cutting back. Laila and I are back to normal. It's like nothing ever happened - good. It's better this way.

That's it, it was a pretty short week. See you soon. Love you and miss you.

Love Peter

It had always been important for Peter to be a loyal and trustworthy friend, and he expected the same in return. Consequently, he was upset with Sean for treating friends in a disrespectful manner. Nevertheless, Peter did not see fighting as a means to resolve a conflict, and I felt assured that he would not kick Sean around.

Peter did, however, have a great deal of anger and frustration. During high school he frequently felt like kicking around those students who had been disrespectful toward

Letter 27 – Male Bonding

him or his friends. We repeatedly talked about the meaning of retaliation. I pointed out that striking back could reduce the chance that the antagonist would feel any guilt or remorse. Consequently, by retaliating Peter would not get revenge, but play into the aggressor's hand. Furthermore, when Peter refrained from striking back, he refused to put himself on the same level as his attacker. Peter agreed with me, but sometimes wanted to "act out" his anger anyway. I understood that, and together we tried to channel his anger and frustration into more socially acceptable behavior, such as exercising or just "talking" it out.

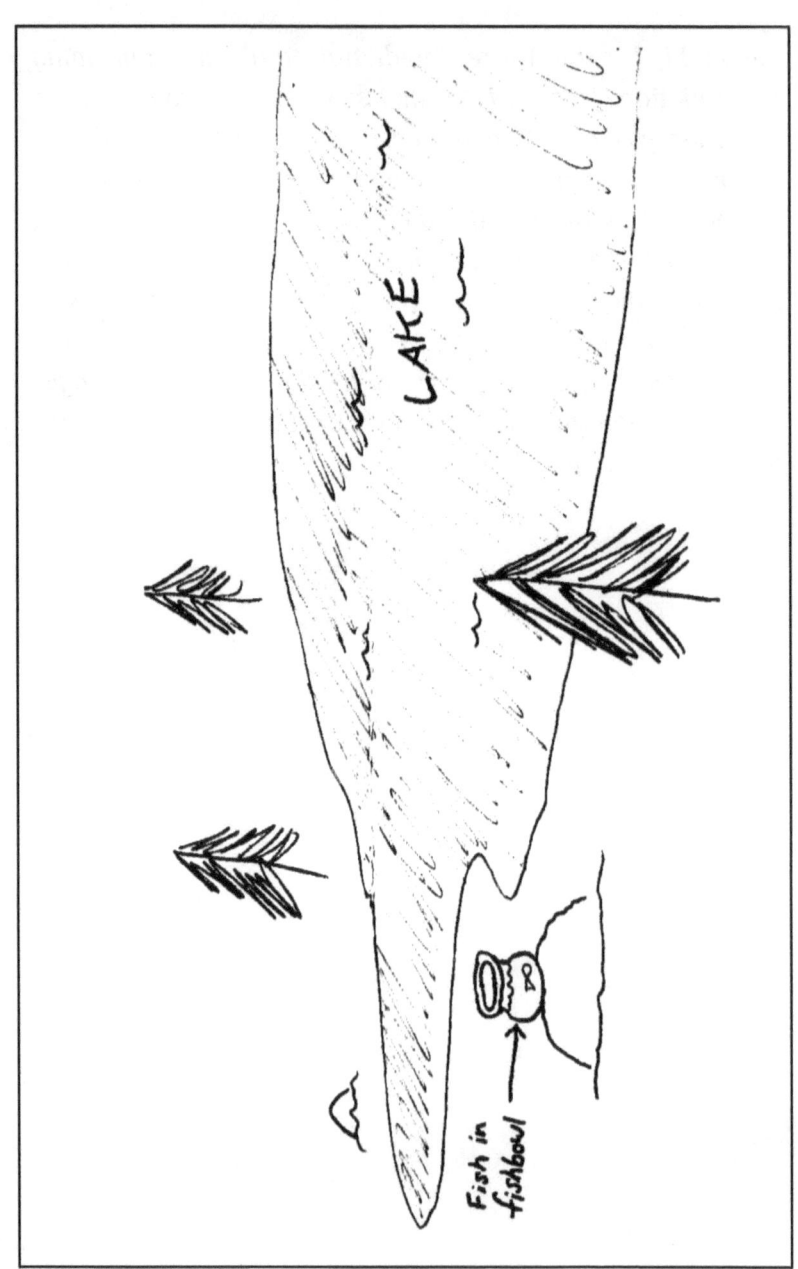

Letter 28 – Senioritis, Again

Peter and I are very much alike, but take issue on some important matters. This is partly because of our different cultural backgrounds, personal histories, and a generation gap. I learned early in life not to be a quitter, and was rewarded for my tenacity. Peter was a perfectionist, and when he was unable to do a project perfectly, or learn quickly, he often lost interest and quit. Being less than perfect was painful for Peter. Unfortunately, he was very hard on himself. He wanted to be a "hero," the one who made up for the shortcomings of his father and myself. He had taken on an impossible task, and over the years we have had many discussions about his fear of being imperfect.

May 6

Dear Mom,

Well, here it is, after I don't know how long. Sorry it has been so long since I last wrote, but at least I called, so look at it that way. Thanks for all your letters Mom, and thanks for all the money, too. I am trying like crazy to save as much as I can. Dad finally sent me some money, so that helped me out a lot. I spend the $200 you sent me. I bought four shirts, two pairs of boxers, and three pairs of shorts. I wear boxers now, because all the guys make fun of me for wearing "grandpa" underwear. Anyway, thanks again, that really saved my butt.

Well, it has finally hit me – SENIORITIS. This is like double, because it's the second time I've been a senior. It's driving me nuts. I want to get on with my life (college, girls, money), but I have to finish up here first. I feel like a fish in a fishbowl sitting on a rock next to a large lake. Do you understand? Oh well, I'm almost done, and I know the last few weeks here will be a blast!

Well, here is some bad news. Jess' grandpa died last Friday. He was pretty bummed, so I didn't do anything this weekend since Jess spent the whole weekend with his grandma, and I didn't want him to feel like he missed out on stuff this weekend. His dad arrived yesterday, so that made him feel better, now I get to meet his dad, too. Gosh, the weird thing is, I got that letter you sent me (the one that said "don't quit") right after I heard about Jess' grandpa's death and it hit me all wrong. See, I know you are upset that I quit Japanese and track. But hell, sometimes peoples' interests change and it's just not worth the trouble anymore. It is better to go on to other things. What is the point in fighting your whole life for something you don't want anymore? I still liked Japanese, but I couldn't respect the teacher and the class anymore. I was getting grades I didn't deserve, what was the point? Why should I get pissed off every time I went to that class when I could pick it up again some time later, in college maybe. As for track, shit, I started much too late to even try being an athlete. I was only out there to see what was going on. I never won a single competition, and that isn't good for my ego, it's like banging my head against a wall, what's the point. Besides, I was pulling the rest of the team down, in all the other events we would at least place, but not shot-put. Get my point? I'm not a quitter just because my interests change. Anyway, the rest of your letter was good, and I will try to keep up that fighting spirit, OK.

Letter 28 – Senioritis, Again

Well, things are pretty much over with Sean. Jess and I talked to him about it and he said, "I don't care, I have fun." That figures. I don't think he cares about anything. We also talked to Pina, whom he is hitting on now about our decision to drop Sean. First, she got all pissed off, but she regretted it, and she wants to stay friends with us for good. What a shame, such a nice, good-looking girl like Pina is falling for an idiot like Sean now. She likes to help people with their problems. I don't know how many times she's invited me to dinner or offered to loan me money. She's so nice, but she doesn't see that Sean is just looking for attention, and once he gets it, he steps all over her, while saying how much he respects her. Pina has the house all to herself this whole week, and she said I could stay over and eat there if I'd like. I might one day this week. I still haven't been to her house. I heard it is real nice. It's a huge farm house way out in the country with horses and other animals.

The weather here has just been great. Not a cloud in the sky all week. Temperatures from 72–85°, and the sun doesn't go down until 10 PM. This is great!! Now I am all tanned, and most of the scars from the Chicken pox are gone. Everyone is running around in shorts and a T-shirt (or no shirt). All the ladies in the house where I live are running around topless during the day. That was weird for me at first, but I got used to it real quick. It wouldn't surprise me if it snowed once more before June comes around though!

This summer is gonna be great! I'm already starting to think about next summer. First, I have to save like a miser, then, I'd like to do one of two things. 1) Go interrailing through Europe for about a month and a half with some friends from Denmark and from the States. 2) Go to Japan and Singapore or maybe Singapore and Australia. WOW!! What do you think?

I better start winding it down here. I talked to Pia today. She called me. We had a great talk, but you are right, she is not for me. Hell, I wonder if anybody is, even though Ann wrote such a hot letter to me, and I'm thinking about calling her next weekend. I'm still not getting my hopes up.

There are now 26 more days until I see you again, I can't wait. I love you and miss you.

Love Peter

P.S. I shaved off my beard

P.S. A bird pooped on my shoulder today while I was in town. Anja told me that's good luck, how does she figure that?

Peter had always been able to "put himself in another person's shoes". He treated others like he wanted to be treated. When Jess' grandpa died, Peter felt it was inappropriate for him to party. It was this sensitivity to others that made Peter a good friend.

In turn Peter's friends in Denmark had helped him overcome some of the feelings of loneliness and confusion he experienced there. Peter was initially taken aback by many of the differences between Danish and American culture. For example, Danish women frequently go topless on the beach and in their backyards in the summer time. Peter recovered quickly, however, from seeing topless women in Denmark.

Letter 29 – Separation Anxiety

This was the last letter Peter wrote to me while he was in Denmark. Soon Sam arrived, and Peter was busy entertaining him and preparing for graduation.

Peter also began to experience separation anxiety, which manifested itself through feelings of distrust toward his friends.

May 17

Dear Mom.

Well, here's one of those letters you don't get as often anymore. Sorry I have become such a lazy letter-writer lately. There is just not that much to talk about anymore. Everything is getting kinda lame, parties are all the same, I've given up on girls in this country, so nothing new in that department either. Actually, this has been one of those weeks (just like last week). I don't know what it is, but something is just eating away at me, everything is bugging me and I'm not trusting anyone. I feel they are all out to get me, even Gudrun. You know what occurred to me today? Things just haven't been right since I shaved my beard off. I also had a nightmare the other night. I was back in the States, and I guess it was winter time and that creepy little Santa Claus doll that I hate, was doing all kinds of scary things, like talking, throwing things, and running around. Anyway, I was getting real scared, and I had it in a position where I could kill it, but you, mom, wouldn't let me, even though you saw it do all those scary things. Anyhow, I can't give all the details, because it was one of those dreams that are so bizarre that you can't even remember all of it. If you have any answers or interpretations tell me, OK, so I can get back to normal.

Only 15 days until you are here. I can't believe it. I only have three more school days. That is great too. I can't wait till you are here (14 days, 16 hours, 20 minutes, and 7 seconds left).

Thanks for the picture of Nila. She looks great. I really hope she wins that contest, as hard as she has worked for it, she deserves it. GOOD LUCK TO HER!

You have probably already guessed, I still haven't received the package you sent. That makes me so mad, because these days that package is all I need to make my week. Damn postal service. Oh yes, and before I go mom, good for you to do so well on your final. Now just keep working harder and no more ditching!!! Ha Ha !!

I better go, I've got so many letters to write. I have been putting it off for about two weeks.

Love Peter

Peter, Nila, and I frequently discussed the meaning of our dreams. When Peter had a nightmare about "that creepy little Santa Claus," he wanted help understanding the dream. The Santa was an antique Danish doll Peter's great grandmother had given him when he was six years old. It did not look like a modern fat and happy Santa. It was a long, slender rag doll with blue pants, a red jacket, and a

Letter 29 – Separation Anxiety

porcelain face. It had a beard and a long Santa hat, and its eyes looked ominous. Peter never liked it and often asked me to get rid of it. I thought his dream about the Danish Santa doll reflected his separation anxiety.

I had just finished another semester at the university, and Peter congratulated me in his letter. He had always been proud of me for going to school, while working and taking care of him and Nila. When he introduced me to his friends in Copenhagen, he proudly showed me off, and I enjoyed feeling appreciated.

Conclusion

When I arrived in Copenhagen, Peter was waiting at the airport. We were very happy to see each other. I met most of Peter's Danish friends, and spent a lovely afternoon with Gudrun and Peter in the famous Danish amusement park, Tivoli Garden. Gudrun was as sweet and mature as Peter had described in his letters. Peter and I took long walks in Copenhagen and its surrounding forests and parks. We talked about his experiences in Denmark, and how they had changed his outlook on life. I showed him pubs that I used to go to when I was his age, and he showed me those he enjoyed that had been established after I moved from Denmark. It was a strange experience for me. I used to be the "authority" on Copenhagen; and now he was the one showing me around.

We stayed with Anja a couple of days. Then Peter, Sam, Jess, and I took off to my father's house in the country, west of Copenhagen. The four of us took walks in the countryside. I showed them the little pond where I learned ice skating. We saw the fields I skied over to get to school when the snow was too deep for walking. We saw my first small school, the one with only one classroom, where I had been the only girl among seven boys. They enjoyed the tours but soon were ready to move on.

I borrowed my father's car and drove around the country with the boys. We visited my relatives in Jutland, a large peninsula bordering on Germany to the west of Copenhagen. Sjaelland,

Adolescent Abroad

the island where Copenhagen is located, is Denmark's largest island. Between Jutland and Sjaelland is another island called Fyn, the childhood home of the storyteller Hans Christian Andersen. In order to get from Copenhagen to Fyn, we needed to take a ferry. Peter had taken that trip with Nila and I several times, and he enjoyed those trips. On Fyn, we saw Hans Christian Andersen's museum, and small villages with thatched roofs and cobblestone streets. We picnicked in the woods and enjoyed the white nights in Jutland. Peter appreciated my efforts as a tour guide, and I enjoyed spending time with those spirited and well behaved young men. The trip was a success, but everything good comes to an end. Soon it was time to part and fly back to the U.S. where distances are large and it would be difficult for the four of us to meet again.

www.ingramcontent.com/pod-product-compliance
Lightning Source LLC
Chambersburg PA
CBHW030052100526
44591CB00008B/123